LYING DOWN
WITH
DOGS

LINDA CARADINE

For information contact:
Unsolicited Press

Portland, Oregon
www.unsolicitedpress.com
orders@unsolicitedpress.com
619-354-8005

Cover Design: Kathryn Gerhardt
Editor: S.R. Stewart

ISBN: 978-1-956692-86-0

TRUTH AND THE ART OF MEMOIR

These are the facts as I remember them. If any event or description is inaccurate, it is because my memory is fallible. Recall is a process linked to personal agenda, to some extent, and the details that resonate with each one of us are dependent on their direct import to us. That is, if I say that Mary was a fat woman with red hair and big feet, you may remember only that Mary is a terrific joke teller. Hence, her physical description is either flawed, misremembered or doesn't have any residual meaning for the reader. I make this distinction because I know I can count on certain people to believe that (1) I am talking about them when I'm not, or (2) because other people will almost certainly dispute the facts as given.

I have tried to tell the complete truth except where I have changed names and physical descriptions in order to protect peoples' privacy. I'm not trying to make anyone look bad, except myself in some circumstances, but I had to include an element of personal history to better illustrate my own journey to the present. In doing so, I can say with confidence that I have not purposefully misrepresented any of the content of this book.

These are my thoughts and opinions. I have attempted to recall details, interactions and observations as they actually took place. The only liberties I have taken have been those that do not affect the overall narrative, i.e., I may have changed the color of a shirt or the name of a restaurant, but the essence of what happened is true to the best of my ability to recollect it. Memory being subjective, I can only say that I have worked hard to recreate events as they actually occurred.

I have not written this book to offend or hurt anyone in any way. It was necessary to convey certain details in order to illustrate my state of mind and/or the actions I took at the time. I have done my best to protect the privacy of all people involved. I have been corrected on some points of fact and chronology and to that I can only say that this book represents my truth.

LYING DOWN
WITH
DOGS

LINDA CARADINE

INTRODUCTION

LYING DOWN WITH DOGS: THE STORY OF OTHER MOTHERS

I won't try to convince you that starting an animal rescue organization is rocket science. It was, in fact, a labor of love. I did it. You can do it, too. Whatever your passion, I give you license to jump in with both feet. In fact, I insist. There's something empowering about following one's muse. It allowed me to find a power within myself that I didn't know I possessed. It allowed me to find love in my heart where I didn't know it existed.

I want to share with you what it was like when I first hatched the idea to start Other Mothers Animal Rescue and when I encountered challenges along the way, the exhilaration of saving one tiny life and the heartbreak of failing to. I want you to know that it has all been worthwhile. There are days when I would rather stay in bed. And there are moments when there's no place else I'd rather be than extricating a half-drowned kitten from a storm drain or sitting up all night with a laboring pit bull.

The challenge is this: No matter how singular our vision, no matter how determined and focused one may be on the end result, life happens along the way. We become distracted, disheartened and disinclined to continue with our endeavors. Sometimes our challenges are small and sometimes they are literally matters of life and death. But we have to push on. We have to keep living and striving for the things we believe are important.

More than anything, I want to show you that we are each the culmination of every experience in our life. No matter what you have done or what you have been through, you can thank every mistake and misadventure for who you are today. Putting it mildly, I had a traumatic childhood. Without that experience, I'm convinced I wouldn't be the person I am now. And though I'm not a great person, I am a decent one.

I first began to write this book as a memoir, striving to capture and enumerate every bump along the way to starting Other Mothers, starting in childhood and culminating in – TA DA! – the realization of my dream. After I finished that first draft, I realized that what I want to share with you is not so much about me and more about how you can do this too. I scrapped the strict memoir format and started all over again. What follows is the story of Other Mothers Animal Rescue. I am a part of it although I guess you can also say that it is a part of me. Unavoidably there are memoir-ish aspects to my tale. Try not to dwell on them as I have myself chosen not to. They are important to the story but they are not the story.

The story is about the animals. You could substitute anyone's life details for my own and still come up with the same results. This is a story of one person's small effort to save animals and, to an extent, what they learned along the way. Mostly, it is about how marvelous the animals were and are – how beautiful, how resilient, how miraculous – all the things we wish we could be ourselves. And they make it look so easy. It is a tribute to all the animals that have passed through my life and a testimonial to their healing nature.

SCRAPPING THE MEMOIR

Last night I told Klaus that I was thinking of scrapping my memoir. As an elder sibling, he should have some insight into this decision, but I had to supply reasons more than that it seemed like the right thing to do. I told him there was a sub-genre known as misery lit and I didn't want to occupy that space. It was not that my agonies weren't real or my scars not evident. I just wasn't sure anymore, now that the tome had written itself to completion, that I wanted or needed to air so much laundry.

"Too whiny, huh?" was all Klaus could manage. Terseness, I suppose, can be a gift.

I was sorely neglected as a child and my school years were torture. I was pursued by the deaths of all the people whom I loved as an adult. It would make interesting reading. Some people might even find strength in my experiences. But, somehow, it all seemed to miss the point that life could be glorious despite all my impressions. To some greater or lesser degree, I had managed to overcome the worst of my traumas. If I'm being honest, I should admit that, on a good day, wearing too much lipstick and failing to lose that final fifteen pounds are among the darkest clouds of times gone by. Like the long shadows that crawl out into the open once a day, there are periodic tears and panic attacks and fretful late-night hours that still plague me. Perhaps most people, or at least most women, have such a story to tell. Did anyone ever really have a happy childhood?

Klaus took my comments under consideration. Or at least I think he did. His coming of age was apparently much more straightforward and prosaic than my own. For me, nothing was ever simple. Nothing followed a hero's journey. Now it appeared the creation of my memoir was another painful and time-consuming misstep in this writer's life. Perhaps the exercise of writing it all down was therapeutic. I didn't think so. I believe I just managed to dredge up a load of angry, ugly memories, and brought them back to life to gnaw at me for a second time. Why was everything so difficult? And why did I feel the need to expose those difficulties all over again? Was this a legitimate use of my talent as a writer? Or was it just, in Klaus's words, too whiny?

Let us be real. Life is not a picnic. It's full of grief and disappointment and all manner of monstrous episodes. But among the thorns there are tiny snatches of contentment, beauty, and joy. For every epithet that was hurled at me as a fat girl in a thin world, there would come a little light into my beleaguered life. Maybe a teacher would compliment my composition. Maybe a boy would look my way. Maybe there would be pizza for lunch. And then the darkness would descend again. As a kid, I came to savor these bright spots and surely that ability helped me to survive. Did I carry a special gene for resiliency or coping that others did not? If so, perhaps that capability should be further developed.

My education faltered. My marriage failed. My career imploded. I believe I've visited some of my own emotional demons on my daughter. Almost everyone I cared about has died. But I've taken some wild trips, rescued a lot of dogs, and read a lot of great books. Those are the things that buoyed me through the years and those are the things that I should feature when I tell about my life. At least I think so.

The problem is, I don't want to come across as some Suzy Sunshine who's never had any challenges. I don't want to sour the depths of my life by looking at it through those tinted glasses. It's much more interesting to color my tale with threads of the mental illness that has grown up with me. It's much more fascinating to delve into what formed me into the person I am. And, to be sure, most all of those formative episodes were ugly and painful.

Let us make a deal. I won't ignore my torment, but I won't overuse it either. A little horror goes a long way.

When I was eight years old, my pet chicken was torn to shreds by an ill-tempered dog. I still cry when I think about that. But do you want to know all about it? Do you need to feel the terror that erupted from my chubby chest when I witnessed the carnage? I'm not sure. I believe that experience was central to my ongoing compassion for the suffering of animals. And that's a good thing. At least it's a good thing when channeled into action. And I believe I have done that for a good part of my adult years. Should I be glad it happened? Meh.

Difficulties. They are learning experiences. There's no question about it. They are opportunities to make choices. They are platforms from which one can leap off into learning and progress. Years of therapy has taught me that we can all make something good of the raw clay of our misery.

At sixteen, I snuck into a St. Louis dive bar and had a night to remember with forty-something rock and roll legend Chuck Berry. Was I a victim of sexual abuse? The experience stays with me as one of the most fortunate, most edifying nights of my life. One person's trash is indeed another person's treasure.

I've traveled the world and seen amazing sights. Some things are just *good*. No two ways about it. But I find that most of life is made of more ambiguous stuff.

In my forties, I had weight loss surgery and a face lift. More than improving my looks, which those procedures did, they taught me a lot about who I really am. I suppose I could have learned to like myself in a less painful way. But that was my process. That's how I did it. Did I mention the surgery was botched and came close to killing me? Did I include the fact that the plastic surgery threw me into bankruptcy?

When I was fifty, I went through a nervous breakdown. I couldn't work any longer. I could scarcely function at all. But that turned out to be the transformative event of my adult years. I wound up ditching my corporate existence and instead pursuing my passions. I started an animal rescue organization. I reconnected with my writing. Falling apart in a very public forum is not for the faint of heart. But it served its purpose.

I'm giving you a thumbnail sketch of some of my challenges in life. These are some of the things that made me who I am today. And I assure you the same is true in your own life. You might choose to write a memoir and plumb the depths of your own problematic issues. I've choosen to skip the details and get right to the good part. The good part, in my case, was how I emerged from the chaos a better person. The good part is looking back, at the age of sixty-five, and feeling that I've evolved just a little bit of irony.

When Klaus looks to me to make sense of our world and our choices now, I can only shrug my shoulders. I don't have any answers. I just have what works for me and a solid understanding of lessons learned.

I am a depressive. But I am a depressive with a positive outlook. I have to be that to survive. It's not an attitude so much as it is the dogged knowledge that, whatever happens, no matter how much life hurts, the view will change. That may be the key kernel of insight that I carry with me from day-to-day walking in this craggy landscape. Ferdinand de Saussure had it right all along: Time changes all words. And life itself is a lot like the language of which he spoke. There are right ways and wrong ways to do it, there are certainly quirks and dialects specific to different peoples and even different individuals, but the bottom line is to be understood and, more so, to understand oneself.

The next time one of my writing buddies asks me how the memoir is coming along, I will simply tell them that it is complete. I have written it from beginning to end with all its excruciating filler. I have coaxed it and vetted it to a fine portrayal of a life with all its warts. I have placed it lovingly in a drawer unless or until the day comes when I feel the need to share it with the world. It is my reflection on life so far and, to be honest, I feel there are already sections that require revision. It is no longer an encapsulation of the authentic me. It is but a fragment of who I was at one time and that slice of life is already, if not obsolete, then blurred and inexact.

Let the years come and change my words and send in the clowns.

A WEEK AGO WEDNESDAY

I hit the pothole with a jolt. The front of the Honda bounced up into the air and the pile of crates in the backseat went flying. In front, my purse dumped a pile of make-up and dog treats onto the floor. I grimaced at the presumed damage to my undercarriage. It was a typical day. I was racing to get the puppies to the vet by 7 a.m. for their spay/neuter appointments. I had to get gas, drive through the bank and do a Fred Meyer stop before going back home to load the little ingrates into their crates for the drive to the vet clinic. Once all the preliminaries were accomplished and I had the pups loaded, I was finally on my way at 6:45. Fortunately, my luck held and no one barfed or had diarrhea before we got there.

I had taken all my meds that morning and was feeling strong. Hydrocodone for my back pain. Adderall for concentration. Potassium for my electrolytes. Losartan and Hydrochlorothiazide for my blood pressure. A B-12 shot to help with my cognitive abilities. Trintellix and Abilify for the depression. Yes, I was ready to face my day. I careened into the parking lot without upending a single puppy. I'd made it on time with seconds to spare.

Betsy, the receptionist, was there to greet me, taking each one of the seven crates in turn and parking them back in the kennel room. I completed the requisite paperwork and flew back down the steps to my car. Maybe I should stop for a coffee. It was going to be a hectic day. I had to run a ton of errands and be back to pick up the puppies before the clinic closed at 5.

My first stop was Annette's house where I needed to check on a pregnant dachshund. I knocked and she called me in. Standing in front of the refrigerator, she was just opening a packet of artisanal gruyere that I assumed was fresh from the Wednesday farmer's market. Its makers were probably a wonderful lesbian couple who free-ranged their herd of Malawian-cross goats in the clovered fields of the fecund Willamette Valley. Happy goats make superior cheese, they had told her. She pulled together of quick salad of GMO-free kale, quinoa and chia seeds and applied a small dab of the gruyere to each of six hand-milled spelt crackers. The morning spread was a splendid locavore feast and she took a moment to thank Gaia for our abundance.

I live in Portland. This was a normal day. It's probably the only place on earth where I could do what I do. Portlanders happen to worship shelter dogs even more than organic and unrefined cuisine.

We were going to have to go by Powell's aptly named City of Books to find the new Wiccan cookbook put out by the local publishing collective. No time like the present, Annette thought, finishing her food. She wedged her hemp-hosed feet into a favorite pair of Birkenstocks, and we set off for the world's greatest bookstore. She wouldn't be caught dead in a Barnes and Noble. Those huge conglomerates were ruining the world. Thank the Goddess we lived in an enlightened city where people knew the enemies of green America. She swished up to her foyer altar, looking down to admire the raw linen wrap skirt she had just bought from that lovely Kenyan woman at the market. She could also wear it as a baby sling or a headdress. The kente cloth was magnificent and bold. On her small table altar sat a brick-sized natural wax eucalyptus candle, a bundle of sage for burning, a couple of quartz crystals and a large piece of healerite stone. She grasped the stone and felt its amazing energy. Her chakras were already feeling better than average.

You see, in Portland, living was an art. We did it freeform in any style we wished. All eccentrics were welcomed here. The right way was any way so long as there were certain common values involved. Number 1: Must love dogs.

Owning her womanstrength, Annette headed for the door and we set off for the bookstore. We had forgotten that today was Flood the Streets with Art Day. Several local craftspeople were participating by leaving free pieces of art at bus stops, on park benches and in other public spaces to make people happy and remind them not to support mass marketing. She spotted a surrealistic two-foot horse rendered in wire and twigs galloping across the steps of Cupcake Connie's pastry shop and decided to leave it for the next art lover. Free art - what a beautiful gesture. Annette said she would have to enroll in a collage workshop or an art glass class so she could contribute next year.

People brought their dogs with them everywhere. There were dog-friendly eateries and brew pubs throughout the city. And once word got out that if you could get your physician to write a letter saying you needed the companionship of your dog for health benefits, you had it made. They couldn't keep you out of any business in town.

Once at Powell's, I noticed a crowd gathered in the Gender Studies aisle. Two fabulous transgender people were arguing loudly over a signed copy of "My Uterus, My Universe." There must have been an author reading earlier in the afternoon. I wandered over to the crossword puzzle section while Annette hurried on to Alternative Spirituality. She was scanning the stacks for Wiccan cookbooks when she almost bumped into another woman with a small baby in her arms.

"OMG, Lyric, is it *you?* I haven't seen you since Cloud Spencer's celebration of life for her pug Bentley. How are you doing?"

"I'm awesome. Just got a massage at that new shiatsu place over on Baker Avenue. Have you met my baby, Smile? She's very social for six months." She flapped the arm holding her baby in Annette's direction. "My doula said Smile has an amazing chi. Can you feel it?"

Annette lifted her eyes heavenward to take a reading. "Of course I can feel it. It's very powerful. How wonderful! Have you had her chart done yet?"

"Not yet. I'm waiting for the equinox."

"Of course. Of course." Annette nodded knowingly.

I think it's clear what was happening around here. A bit of exaggeration? Well, perhaps. But Annette and Lyric were both real Portlanders and they sounded just like that to me. The main point here, to which I alluded earlier, was that Portland is in love with rescue dogs, the scruffier and more downtrodden the better. We didn't have a lot of traditional god believers here in the Rose City so a typical Sunday might revolve around going to a shelter to adopt a special needs pet. All hail the higher power of Dog.

In Portland, a person who buys a home and uses it as a halfway house for pregnant animals was not strange at all. I fit right in. And that was a big part of my own healing process. I'd never felt that sense of belonging before. It was ironic. The more different you were around here, the more you were one of the tribe. For once, my weirdness was a good thing.

I had found a route, albeit a circuitous and bumpy one, to doing what I loved and being reasonably happy doing it. Neither my clinical depression nor the scars of my tortured childhood could keep me from what I considered my destiny. But to speak of destiny perhaps took too much away from me and from my own choices in life. I had managed to successfully navigate what was for me a difficult landscape of unattained expectations. Those elusive must-haves of marriage, a corporate career, and graceful aging with grandchildren bouncing on my knee and a song in my heart, were not in the cards. Not for me, none of it.

I had always been an animal lover. I don't know whether that was what made me different than a lot of other people or if the differentness and the animal-loving just happened to coexist. Either way, the path was there. All I had to do was choose to take it. Without even stopping to consider it, I had chosen just the right place to start an animal rescue organization. And I had run it happily for years before the landscape began to change. Portland was still a dog city at the end of the day, but we were succeeding so well in the organization's latter days that such an enterprise was no longer a necessity. People were already choosing to spay and neuter their pets and there were fewer unwanted animals than ever before. We were having to pull our pregnant dogs from farther and farther away, from places where they still had kill shelters and a lack of foster volunteers. I had nearly succeeded myself right out of business. But that was the plan all along – to find homes for all those lovelorn mutts – so I could hardly complain.

I could finally retire from my working life with the sense that I had done something that mattered. Now was the time for me indulge my peripatetic streak with glad abandon. I had already gotten around to several spots on the map – from

China to South America and all over Europe – but there were countless places still on my list. Now, for once in my life, I had both the time and the money to venture out without worrying about my job going unmanned or the bills getting paid while I gallivanted.

I was in the midst of planning a New York City tour when the pandemic hit. Wasn't it amazing the curve balls life can throw at you? I mean, who could have foreseen this? Instead of jetting off for a fortnight of shopping and Broadway plays, I was stuck at home in my robe watching reruns of Divorce Court and ordering toilet paper on the internet. Ironic indeed

I could scarcely anticipate an end to this. Would the virus burn itself out and leave the survivors as it found us? Would the universe provide an effective, readily available vaccine? Or would we all be changed to think about life in some extraordinary new ways? And when would it happen? The daily news sought to convince us that the "reopening" was imminent, but I didn't know how that could be. Covid-19 would surely be with us for the foreseeable future. Where once I found my city environment unique, I now saw that we were the same as those in Dallas and Peoria and Indianapolis – all of us snared in the worldwide web of the coronavirus and waiting for something to happen. And something *would* happen, that much was inevitable. The planet was vast enough and humankind resourceful enough that those malignant and infinitesimal lifeforms among us would be dealt with, maybe not once and for all, but partially and for a while at least.

I may yet make it to New York and to places beyond. I could only wait and hope that my old life, the good life, would be restored. In the meantime, I had a puppy room to clean in anticipation of the little ones returning home from the clinic, a hundred or so phone calls to make and a new strategy to develop on how to rescue even more pregnant dogs.

IN THE BEGINNING

Three months before John F. Kennedy was assassinated riding in a Lincoln Continental convertible in Dallas, Texas, I was a bashful six-year-old arriving in a white Plymouth Belvedere at my new home in DeRidder, Louisiana. Just another west Louisiana one-stoplight town, it was near Fort Polk and that was enough to lure my army family. Once again, we were looking for yet another inexpensive rental house within proximity to my dad's latest post. I didn't know who JFK was, or what his presidency meant. This was my seventh new home in as long as I could remember and I was consumed with more immediate matters. Would I make any new friends? Would I be allowed to have a pony? Would my chicken have a house of her own?

Small town Louisiana in 1963 was a virtual hell hole of flagrant ignorance and racism. Our next-door neighbors who brought over get-acquainted casseroles were the same family that had a black cat named Nigger. Strangely, it was a place I came to love. Lacking any kind of purposeful guidance in such matters, what I knew then was that some kids came to school without shoes and that there was no shame in being poor so long as you were white. I knew that the colored ladies lowered their heads and stepped off the sidewalk to get out of the way of my mom or any other white lady on her way to the Hinky Dinky five-and-dime on Main Street. I knew they had their own school and their own town that we never visited. On the map, it was called Sugartown, but that wasn't what everyone called it. They even had their own drinking fountains and special doors in cafes. They owned the balcony at the Joy Theater and I wasn't allowed up there even though I wanted to go.

It didn't occur to me to question these things, or any other things, beyond the extent to which they affected me. And they did not affect me, so I didn't wonder and I didn't ask. Although my parents didn't actively participate in the derogatory name-calling and hateful rants, they never condemned it. And my mom didn't hesitate to take me with her when she gathered up her cigarette case and six-pack of cold Pepsi and walked up the gravel road to visit the neighbors. In her flowered sundress, she had freckles across her shoulders. Her bare limbs were strong and willful as she strode along purposefully with me running in her wake.

The family next door, the Houstons, had two teenage sons and had built the little frame house in which we now lived. The mom chain-smoked Winstons and raised Chihuahua dogs for extra money. The dad was big and blustery and seemed especially outraged about the Negroes. He was the town sheriff.

Another family was named Freeman and they lived up at the turn-around in the road in a nicer, bigger brick house. In time, the daughter, who was a lot older than me, would allow me to ride her horse, Trigger. The Freemans belonged to a strange church called Pentecostal that said girls should never cut their hair or wear shorts. They were a little different from the rest of us, neither snubbed nor scorned, but somehow removed from those who lived along the road.

Of course I didn't know any of this on the day we arrived in the Plymouth. I only knew I was anxious to get out and walk my chicken. We had gone to see my Grandma on our way south from Springfield, Missouri, and through Oklahoma where she lived on a real farm. To me, an avid animal lover, that was the Promised Land. She had cows and pigs and chickens and dogs called Beagles. My Grandma told me if I could catch one of the little chicks, I could take it with me when we left. I managed to corner a fluffy one and put it into a shoe box along with some grass and a handful of chicken feed. I had taken one of my colored pencils to poke holes in the top of the box so my chicken could breathe.

I loved that little chick and took the box with me into stores and cafes and motel rooms all the way to DeRidder. I was a morbidly shy little girl without any lasting friends or attachments. But I had a chicken and a prodigious imagination and a passion for animals, all of which I carried with me wherever I was taken.

When the Plymouth came to a stop in front of the unpainted little house on a dirt road in backwoods Louisiana, it was all I could do not to shout with glee. Filled with the wonder of a naïve little girl, I burst out of the car with my peeping shoebox and my high hopes about the shantytown animal empire that I hoped to build.

While the adults toured the house and Klaus went off down the road to kick at rocks, I found an abandoned doghouse around back that I fancied would make a lovely new home for my chicken. Only it wasn't abandoned, and the tenant, a very pregnant and ill-tempered Chihuahua named Roxie, came running as fast as her little legs could carry her and chased my chicken around the side of the house. By the time I caught up with them, there was little left but blood and feathers. Roxie turned on me and barked a couple of times before running off toward the house next door.

That was the first cogent memory I have of caring about the welfare of animals. It was self-serving and limited in scope to the bloody death of one tiny chick. But it was the beginning and the rest sprawls out through the years as I got my first dog, collected box turtles, had cats and rabbits and birds and horses and practically every other creature that existed. The part that always stayed with me was caring for them and protecting them. That's apparently what I was meant to do. And it took me fifty years to take that simple destiny and run with it.

The other part of that early experience was my first stroke of awareness that my family wasn't like other families, or at least not like I thought other families should be. Mine either didn't care about me or were unable to show their love. The result was the same. I grew up unguided and unregarded. There was no comfort brought to me about the death of my chicken, no concern about the effect yet another move would have on an already painfully shy child, neither an explanation of bigotry that my young ears would make sense of. Only silence. Silence and expectation. They always expected me to be if not upstanding or correct, then appropriate for every circumstance that came my way.

****

Growing up the way I did, relatively unnoticed and splashed into and out of diverse environments every year or two when my dad was transferred by the army and, later, by his second career in federal civil service, I'd become something of a budding sociopath. I didn't actively manipulate or violate the rights of others but I held a total disregard for social norms and I masked my true feelings and intentions because I believed I was different from other people.

I did what was expected of me, no more and no less, kept my dreams to myself, remaining utterly apart and alone. Friends, and later lovers, came into my life and it didn't faze me when they ultimately went away. And they all did go away. I expected it. I longed for it, longed for an end to the complications of a peopled life. I wanted to stay in my room, writing or just daydreaming, searching everywhere for that perfect life that had so far eluded me.

I can remember these dreadful family vacations we used to embark on every summer. No, not to Wally World. That would have been a dream come true. Instead, we drove around the country visiting relatives we didn't know and doing it as cheaply as possible. The strategy involved "making incredible time" by day, stopping only for six-for-a-buck hamburgers at some greasy spoon drive-in along the way. I can still hear my mother chastising me about wanting to have cheese or fries with my burger. Extras were strictly *verboten*.

"No fries," she would say. "You don't need fries." As a fat kid, that always had a special zing to it. I didn't realize she was just trying to save money. At least that was part of it.

We timed each nine- or ten-hour spell of driving so we could arrive at the relatives' homes in time to stay the night. A lot of them were rural people. They didn't have spacious houses. Some of them didn't even have indoor bathrooms. But they were all welcoming. Just as if this was normal behavior. What I remember most is hiding on the porch or out in the barn while the grown-ups sat chatting and getting acquainted. I literally ran from these people. I don't know why my mom and dad didn't realize this was abnormal behavior even for a little kid.

The next day, after a night sleeping on the floor with some kids I didn't know and to whom I refused to say a word, we would start out again at daybreak. Klaus and I stretched out in the back of the station wagon. He was intent on finding new ways to make me cry while I just longed for the inevitable stop when I could get out of the car for a few minutes and partake of a greasy hamburger.

"Go to the bathroom. And come right back." That was the drill. "No, you can't have fries. You don't need any fries."

There still exists today a gallery of photos of Klaus and me as little children, all dressed up in our Easter best or togged out in mismatched corduroy trousers and shirts, looking for all the world like we were the Children of the Corn. Haunted. Vacant-eyed. In every photo but one we both appeared as if we were suffering from some kind of post-traumatic stress disorder. The exception is one where I'm about five or six and happily eating an ice cream cone.

****

I was *that* kid, the one with a huge bullseye painted on my chubby chest. I attracted playground bullies, mean girls, teachers with cruel streaks, and all manner of thugs in training. *Lord of the Flies* was the story of my life. I was the kid who would start to cry at the slightest provocation. And those tears were like blood in the water. If it's true that there's something primal in the hunt, then someone will always be the prey. Sometimes prey does escape, and I did, but not without my scars.

Through all the times we moved and all of my early agonies, my dad was away, being "in the army" and stationed in strange-sounding places. Though the Second World War was long over, it was still alive and well in my family, and all word of it came through my mother's eyes. She told us about being at home in Leipzig with her stern parents and many sisters and of hearing the bombs dropping on their town. She told us repeatedly of escaping East Germany after the war, of being shot at, of bribing the Russian guards with bottles of cognac, of running for her life. She was a German war bride. To her, evidently, meeting my dad was not so much of a love story as a tale of redemption. She got to come to America.

The story of my mother's war explained a lot of things. I got the feeling the way our lives played out was just a byproduct of her acting the parts of housewife and mother and citizen, of doing all the right things to avoid being snatched away in the middle of the night by the Gestapo. It seemed normal from the outside but, to me, inside and looking out, my childhood seemed to exist in a vacuum. There was no context to it at all. I was playing a part too and felt that I wasn't quite as good at my role as I should have been. No one ever complained or told me to be a better daughter and sister, but their dissatisfaction with me was there just the same.

My mother would say "This is good enough" as an answer to any complaint I might have about my cheap and raggedy school clothes, the food I took for my lunch, or my poor general potential in life. "This is good enough" meant you were lucky you didn't live behind the Iron Curtain. "This is good enough" meant you were foolish and misguided to ask for or expect more of anything. Whether this had to do with a limited family budget or just a cheap, miserly world view, I didn't know. The results were the same. I longed for something I didn't have and I couldn't put a name on what it was.

I remember one time a representative from the Girl Scouts came to my school to recruit. It sounded like the coolest thing ever so I took my sign-up form home with mounting excitement. My mom said when she was a kid, she wanted to join Hitler Youth and her dad had punished her severely. I guess that meant not being in the Girl Scouts was good enough for me.

My mother's war also meant that she spoke with a pronounced accent people found charming. As I grew older it occurred to me that when people spoke Spanish, for example, or any Asian language, they were told impatiently to "speak English" while my mother continued to charm. Apparently, some accents were better to have than others. In sixty-some years, hers never lessened, never changed. She would come to use it as a reason she didn't understand or remember anything she didn't want to understand or remember. Klaus was born in Germany and spoke German at home as a little kid. By the time I was born, we were in the States. I was given an American name after some B-movie Hollywood starlet and was expected to learn and speak English. This was a tall order for a kid who spent ninety-nine percent of her time with her foreign-speaking mother and brother. English turned out to be one of my favorite subjects once I started school, not because of any accolades I achieved by mastering it against long odds but because I loved the way it sounded. I loved the way it looked on the page. I loved the rules that ordered its usage. Everything about speaking and writing English excited me in a way that little else did when I was small and playing the part of the second child.

I don't ever recall my parents talking with my teachers or involving themselves in the business of my childhood. My dad was simply away most of the time and my mom just didn't understand a lot of what was happening. I didn't understand much either but it wasn't a language barrier in my case. It was that odd lack of context that I existed in. No one ever told me what was expected or who I was supposed to be. I was just a little creature made up entirely of emotional reactions. When someone looked at me or spoke to me, I usually just cried. When I look back now, I think of myself as being like one of those feral children raised by wolves. I had just awakened in a strange, new environment and everything terrified me. There should have been someone there to tell me everything was going to be okay.

****

Years passed, as they inexorably do, and I grew up the product of a lifetime of unintentional neglect. Assumptions were corrected, lessons were learned and I came to adulthood in a strange state of wonder. Oh, this is what it all means. I blundered through each compartmentalized aspect of my life – career, marriage, motherhood. By the time I'd reach the cusp of my golden years, I knew not to cry in public if I could help it. I knew that role-playing was not always the answer to fitting in. And I knew that authenticity counted a hell of a lot sometimes.

A DIFFERENT LIFE

Three years before the birth of my first and only child, my now-ex and I came to live in St. Louis in an early twentieth century Italianate apartment building. It was adorned with projecting eaves supported by impressive corbels and an elaborate cornice around its low-pitched roof. We used to think the building was reminiscent of the apartment house Ira Levin had written about in Rosemary's Baby though the reality of our sixth-floor efficiency, with its Murphy bed and built-in bookcases, was much less grand but every bit as haunted.

In the space of my two years in St. Louis, I had managed to graduate from high school and had fallen in love with a man who was as odd as I was. He wrote poetry and had grandiose dreams. We fit together like two peas in the proverbial pod. He didn't seem to realize that I was different from other girls in some basic and irredeemable way. Or it didn't matter to him. Craig was sensitive, tall, and good-looking—everything my prince should be. It didn't matter to me that he was Black and I was white. And it didn't occur to me that anyone else would mind. That's how naïve I was.

My own parents didn't talk to me during this period. I lived in the Black culture of the pre-disco seventies with Craig, his mother, his sisters, his smart-aleck cousin Darnell and his best friend C. Dobbs, all of whom lived within a quarter mile of us. We had bootleg cable TV and bought clothes and fake jewelry out of the trunk of someone's car. We ate carry-out barbeque from a joint with a steel mesh security door. We listened to War on the car radio and stood in line to get government cheese. That was a time when people really did buy a new car when they couldn't afford a decent place to live. This lifestyle came to be known as ghetto fabulous but back in the day it just made sense. If you were poor, you did your hair and nails and had a kickin' ride. It was a way of controlling the things you could control and thumbing your nose at the rest.

Craig and I got married in 1976, the year of our country's Bicentennial. Ours was a sad little ceremony in the basement of a courthouse in downtown St. Louis. My groom wore a wide-lapelled three-piece suit with orange platform shoes, and I wore jeans and a tee shirt. As much as our parents didn't approve of our marrying, I felt I was finally a part of something special.

During our ten years together, we witnessed a police shooting of an unarmed African American youth, had our dog shot by racist neighbors and our suburban Ferguson house burned to the ground by the local KKK, but we lived in a state of bliss. At least I did. I was in love and nothing could touch that.

One afternoon, Craig's younger sister Colette came over. We were taking my rattletrap 1972 Pinto station wagon to see John Carpenter's horror film, Halloween. I liked scary movies and Collette was secretly in love with Donald Pleasance. We went downtown to the Fox Theater where you could still sit in the dark corners and smoke cigarettes during the feature. Michael Myers scared the crap out of us, especially the part where he shimmied up on top of Dr. Loomis's car on the fog-infused grounds of the insane asylum. I still love horror movies, but it was a long time ago that I could scream in sincere terror at a beheading or an eye-gouging. Those were innocent times.

After the movie, we stopped by White Castle for a bagful of sliders to take home to Craig and C. Dobbs. C. Dobbs was no Donald Pleasance but Collette had a crush on him just the same. On this particular evening, he had decided he wanted to jump from our kitchen window two stories to a balcony below us. Whether substance abuse played any part in his decision, I do not recall.

"Hey Dobbs, don't do it." Colette tried.

"C. Dobbs, you a fool, man." Craig tried too.

But he did it anyway, presumably to impress Colette. He ended up landing at a weird angle and sprained his ankle on one of his platform shoes. It was a hell of an anticlimax after having just seen Jamie Lee Curtis evade her crazed stalker. But we appreciated his efforts, glad he didn't hurt himself worse, and wrapped his ankle in an Ace bandage for the ride home.

Although I never heard C. Dobbs himself mention the stunt again, it became the stuff of legend among the rest of us, many of whom weren't even present that night to see it in person.

"Remember the night C. Dobbs jumped off the balcony?" someone would say. And the rest of us would chime in with our own observations or accounts of the event.

Darnell was especially lavish in his praise. "He be Superman. He be flying, man."

"Yeah, cuz. He be *flying*." Craig would add with an appreciative chuckle.

By the time she was twenty-two, Collette had two kids with different dads and lived in Section 8 housing. She was a wise, sweet woman who wanted nothing more than to be married to a nice man and live the 1950's version of the American dream. I don't know why it didn't work out that way for her. She doted on her kids and cooked up elaborate meals for Craig and me on Sundays. She went to play Bingo every month when her welfare check came. She never worked and she never learned how to drive a car. Collette was typical of the women I knew during this time. She was miles away from the fiercely independent, feminist archetype that I had come of age with. I didn't know why, but I was sure there was something culturally significant about this fact. I loved her but I didn't understand who she was.

Maybe the gap was just too wide between she and I, and between Craig and me, to ever be spanned. We really did come from different worlds even though I never thought of myself as having a type or a culture. It was just me, typing in my room, reading Margaret Atwood and Nathaniel

Hawthorne, going out to see Fellini films at the local art house. There was nothing elitist or even studious about me. I just sought out things that were different, unusual. Maybe that's how I wound up living this certain kind of life back in the seventies. Now it seemed so improbable and so far away.

I held on for dear life through a decade of marriage filled with personal outrages any one of which would have spurred most self-respecting young wives to fly the coop. I believed what I wanted to believe, perhaps what I needed to believe. He was unfaithful. I rejected that possibility out of hand. He was drug dependent. I cosseted it in gentler terms of self-medication and non-traditionalism. He was abusive. I was convinced that my own self-improvement was the answer to that. Through all these slings and arrows, I persevered. And when I finally did leave Craig, I knew beyond all reasonable doubt that I was doing the right thing. I never had any second thoughts, never looked back. And there was no one big thing that made me leave. It just took me a long time to accept the writing on the wall. He was no longer the man I fell in love with. Or perhaps I was seeing him without my rose-colored glasses for the first time. Either way, I had to leave.

And I left more behind than a wayward husband. I left behind my willingness to accept less than what I was due. I'd been ignored and underloved all my life. I was done. Never again would someone treat me badly Not a parent. Not a lover. Not anyone. If I had to spend the rest of my life alone, I was through with this. It was too painful. It was too messy.

And I was on to the next chapter in my life. The psychological abuse I endured living with a drug addict was monumental. He had to accuse me, berate me, shame me, and ignore me in order to live with himself, I suppose. But, after all those intense and unsatisfying years, it was over. I was free and eager to run.

****

I tend to think Oregon came to me rather than the other way around. In February 1986, freshly divorced, with a 4-year-old daughter and three cats in tow, I clearly had to go somewhere. Fortunately, for me at least, my brother Klaus lived in some hinterland logging community in central Oregon and I figured that I could get a job in the nearby city of Portland. I took the first one offered to me. Come August I was a computer operator for Ensign Insurance Co. I commuted the 90-mile drive daily for the first few months and then was able to secure an apartment in the city. I found out that I tend to do well when I have to.

Living with Klaus, my daughter and the aforementioned three cats was a revelation. Klaus had a little daughter and a cat of his own. Dinah and I staked out the living room of his small upstairs apartment as our territory. Sleeping bags and cat cages lined the walls. Klaus, not one to invite inconvenience or clutter into his carefully ordered life, never uttered a word of complaint. Not that I can remember, of course. He may have been carping at me from morning to night but I was so intent on making things work that I didn't hear a word of it. I prefer to think he went out on a limb for me.

One morning Klaus was sitting in the open kitchen drinking coffee and working on a crossword. Ten feet away, I was sprawled out on the floor just waking up. If the birds were singing outside, I wasn't hearing them.

"What's a seven-letter word for fall?"

Not one to skip a beat, I asked, "Fall the season or fall the verb? Any letters yet?"

"Dunno. The third letter is a 'u.' At least I think it is." He hadn't yet looked up, his glasses resting halfway down his nose.

"Just don't get too excited and *plummet* from your chair, bro." I replied.

"Of *course*."

"Dork"

"Moron"

This is how we said we loved each other. In my family, you didn't talk about or show your emotions. It was *verboten*. But there were ways to get things across when you needed to. This probably goes a long way in explaining my relative shortcomings in the art of romantic relationships. Men tended to think I was stringing them along and that I didn't really care about them while I was simply perplexed by their seeming neediness. It was to be a recurring theme for years as I desperately wanted to find a lasting partner in life. It was nice to have in Klaus one person who "got me" to some extent.

Still, moving to that first Portland apartment was a welcome change, mainly because I was escaping my long commute. It was a decent two-bedroom in a good school district. We loaded all my crap into a rented truck, and I moved it north to Portland early in 1987.

I landed on my feet somehow, bowed but unbroken. Back in the mid-1980's, Portland was even more of a one-of-a-kind town, a place where people celebrated being different as a kind of personal art. I was happy to struggle through the years it took to raise a child, the way most women do and, lacking practical resources, came to once again embrace the ability to live in a world of my own making.

My little daughter Dinah started school and did well. She was active, smart, and outgoing. She started playing soccer in 1st grade. I can still see her long braids flying behind her as she ran down the field in her cleats and oversized jersey. She was my life and, for the next decade or so, I was content to work and take care of her.

At first, I had some doubts about how Dinah would fare as a biracial child. But she seemed to thrive. She had a diverse group of friends and was excelling in school. I was as proud of her as I could be. She told me later that she didn't know she was different than the other kids until sometime in middle school when some older kid used a racial slur in referring to her. I knew my ex would have disapproved of my not raising Dinah as a Black child in a white world. His racial identity was important to him. And I believe if Dinah had been a boy, I would have been forced to face the issue of race from the perspective of personal safety. This was one thing I wasn't naïve about. I had seen enough hatred and bigotry back in St. Louis to last a lifetime. As it was, race was an open topic, but not one we dwelt on.

I guess I finally and forever fell out of love with Craig when he failed miserably to remain a part of Dinah's life. There were sporadic phone calls, but he made no real effort to forge a relationship with her over the years. There were no child support payments and no visits. As an adult, Dinah would bear a burden of anger toward her father that sputtered into an eventual indifference. She didn't remember being with him and I didn't remember that he had once been "the one," warm and charismatic. I supposed that was the cost a life of drug addiction took on a man's soul. I paid too but, in return, I got something of value. I earned the knowledge that fairy tales don't necessarily come true, that no man was worth giving up on oneself for, and that I was good enough on my own to live in the world.

CAREER ROLLER COASTER

I started with Ensign Insurance in 1986 hot on the tail of what had been an emotionally devastating divorce and smack in the middle of a big, fat clinical depression that robbed me of the ability to concentrate, remember or cogitate. For years at Ensign, I continued to do what I did best which was to apply for new jobs within the company. At some point in time, another hiring manager was fooled into believing I would be an asset to her department. I became a customer service supervisor in a call center. To this day, I am thankful to the woman who hired me for that position. It was away from the computers, for which I had no natural knack, and had a certain management cache complete with a prestigious corner cube. Moreover, the work was general enough that I found I could do this job quite well. My staff was well-established and fairly autonomous, so I didn't really need to know their work. I just walked around spouting corporate lingo and acting like I was in charge. At least that's what it seemed like at the time. In hindsight, I was probably good at this work because I tried to be fair to everyone and was naïve enough not to have a hidden agenda. I took the time to listen to my team and to genuinely look out for their interests. It turned out I had a talent for hiring and cultivating good employees as well.

I often wonder how things would have turned out had I stayed, content and successful, in that job. But that's not the way I operated. When the chance came to be in on the ground floor of a brand-new department, from the hiring of staff to developing new policies and procedures, I couldn't stand by and not throw my hat into the ring.

It was a cruel irony that I was also skillful at clinching interviews and getting new jobs. Once I'd gotten this one, I realized from the first day that I had stepped off into a huge hole. I was smart enough and should have been able to hit the ground running but, because of my lack of focus and, probably, my lack of self-esteem, I started out pretending and soon was hopelessly left behind. I had no idea what I was being asked to do. I am a verbally precise person. If you want me to build a house, say "build a house." They weren't saying that. They were losing me in conversations around "navigation in emotional landscapes" and having meetings about "nimble planning." They knew things I didn't know. They all seemed to be able to intuit what was going on under the surface. They spoke a strange jargon that said everything and nothing at the same time. And though I could talk the talk with the best of them, I was unable to interpret it. For me, the absence of clear direction was a killer. Personally, I now think the secret to my peers' success was risk aversion and side-stepping of accountability. If a project succeeded, they could take full credit. If it failed, they could distance themselves or blame someone else.

Still, it's difficult to accept – and harder yet to admit – to hopeless confusion. Perhaps if I had piped up right at the beginning and asked for help, it would have gone better. But I sat silent through all those meetings, nodding my head and taking notes until it seemed everyone had a clear direction and a common goal. Except me. I tuned out what people were saying and then tried to fake my way into some kind of dubious accord when called upon to contribute to the discussion.

Once they realized that I didn't know what was going on, I didn't even understand that I was being placed on a "coaching plan." If it had been happening to someone else, I would have realized as a manager that this was a final step in documenting a termination. When I finally got the message that my livelihood was threatened, I did what I needed to do to survive. I applied for yet another open position.

This final supervisory slot put me squarely in the path of Shirley, a wily old-school manager who ruled with a take-no-prisoners approach. It was her way or the highway, and she steamrolled right over me. I was charged with the responsibility to step in and deconstruct my new staff to put it back together in a way that would function cheaper and better. I had no clue where to begin and I was defeated before I even started.

I was finally realizing that my depression had a huge effect on my cognitive skills. When I piped up and invoked the Americans with Disabilities Act (ADA) to protect me, Shirley was having none of it. She knew I was an inept fake. And she didn't care why. I was unable to learn the business processes that I was being asked to overhaul. Over and over, I went to my staff for suggestions. Then I would try to implement a new "improved" procedure and I wouldn't be able to defend it to my manager. Shirley wanted to know exactly how and why I was doing what I did. She also did not appreciate all the time I was taking off for doctors' appointments, therapy sessions and just plain old-fashioned mental health days.

I spent my workdays just a comment or a look away from emotional breakdown. The fact that I was frequently running off to the restroom crying did little to instill confidence with my coworkers. The state I was in was probably what used to be called a nervous breakdown. I probably should have been hospitalized at some point to reset my emotions and shore up my defenses. But I plodded on ineffectually until, inevitably, I was called on the carpet. It was only because my manager's tactics were draconian and, hence, introduced some measure of legal liability under the ADA, that I did not lose my job. Somehow, I continued to survive, and was demoted instead to a position equal to those I had been supervising.

This new slot as a claims analyst was not only an obvious and demeaning fall from grace but an even worse application of my capabilities. While I had been able to perform at least some of the less specific, less technical aspects of managing people, I was wholly unable to master the step-by-step processes which I was now asked to perform. I couldn't learn the computer systems, couldn't remember a sequence of events or document my outcomes sufficiently. I was hopeless at mastering the terms of the insurance policies that I was supposed to administer. I was unable to apply supportable logic to my claims decisions.

Again, if I had only been forthcoming from the start about what was happening to me, perhaps I might have been accommodated in some way that would have allowed me to continue doing meaningful work. But that ship had sailed. True, most of my 25 years in service to Ensign Insurance had outwardly been stellar. I had accomplished a lot along the way while I occupied that sweet spot in my first supervisory position. Then came my inevitable downfall into depression that eclipsed all the good I had done.

The final denouement came down to a summons to a conference room on a Friday afternoon. That's a set-up for a death sentence if I ever heard one. There sat Shirley and a couple of smooth talkers from Human Resources whose job it was to facilitate the ugly truth of what was to come. I had to go. Fortunately, I had enough years in to qualify for early retirement. So, they proudly announced my retirement, threw me a party, and showed me the door.

In a way, I never recovered from my fall. But I somehow landed on my feet financially what with a small pension I'd accrued and Social Security Disability benefits. I was 55 years old, ten years from normal retirement age, and I could afford not to think about finding another job, although I did take steps to test my abilities in the coming years by working short-duration temp jobs. These didn't go well and I resigned myself in time to unemployment. Outwardly, I was a successful early retiree, someone who had planned astutely and wound up with a life of leisure. On the inside, though, I was a failure. I doubted every step I took and every move I made. It took me a long time not to feel like an imposter as a retiree when the truth of the matter was that I had been let go from my job for poor performance. Gradually I did learn to accept the fact that I was a symptomatic depressive, someone whose abilities were severely limited by my disorder. It gave me no joy, but it also afforded me little guilt these days that I was so limited. As people say, it is what it is. My roller coaster career came to a stop gently and with a sense of any real danger having been averted.

I left Ensign in 2011, and I was not as well-prepared financially as I had thought. I blew through my savings rapidly, had to file bankruptcy, and was left emotionally unfit to seek any kind of reasonable employment elsewhere. I continued on Disability and set about surviving on a shoestring budget so that I could enjoy life without what felt like a noose around my neck. In a lot of ways it was pretty sweet. Though I didn't have the means to travel, I did now have the time to do a lot of reading and writing and volunteering. Also, I continued with my therapy and the ongoing sampling of every psychotropic drug known to man. Gradually, I began to get my mojo back. Whether it was the right combination of drugs, the time to rest and rehabilitate myself, or just the absence of work stress, I had arrived in a place where I could function again on most days and as long as nothing unanticipated happened. All I needed now was a cause to throw myself into. Reenter my lifelong love of animals.

Since about 2005 I had volunteered off and on for the Oregon Humane Society where I got my regular "fur fix" throughout years of living in apartments with strict no-pets policies. Those pathetic little kittens and sad-eyed dogs were all there for the hugging. I was probably one of the few volunteers they ever had who didn't mind cleaning dirty cages. I did it with love in my heart for every animal that fell into my orbit.

For a while I worked part-time as a vet assistant, helping with treatments and surgeries all day long. The young vet I worked for had swine farmers as clients. This frequently entailed mixing up big batches of E.coli bacteria in powered milk and, every once in a while, doing a piglet necropsy to test the levels of antibiotics in their systems. I don't remember thinking about the E. coli being dangerous or the innocent little pig being sacrificed. All I knew was that I was doing what I most loved – and getting paid precious little for the opportunity.

Of course, I had animals of my own during those years, most notably a group of three similar-looking cats that I reported to the apartment management as one cat, and hoped they never all sat in the window at the same time. I toyed with showing cats for a few years and scraped together enough money to take weekly dressage lessons on a leased horse named Wimples that was a lot better trained for the practice than I was.

I had been rescuing dogs and cats through a loose network of contacts I had made at various local shelters. I learned by sad experience that pregnant females were often subject to euthanasia in conventional shelters, so my practice was to accept only those animals and raise the babies until they were old enough to be spayed and neutered. Then I would find homes for all of them. As an animal lover, it turned into a sort of calling. I bought my first house that year specifically with this work in mind. I decided to start a nonprofit 501(c)3 so I could do this full time, or at least to my personal capacity. I could recruit a bunch of volunteers to raise even more litters than I could handle on my own and I would be able to accept donations from the public.

Once I stopped working in 2011, the sky was the limit. I used LegalZoom for my incorporation, pulled together a board of directors from friends who shared my passion and had some know-how to share, and launched Other Mothers Animal Rescue and Rehabilitation, Inc.

FROM DREAM TO REALITY

Portland, Oregon was inarguably Dogville, USA. The idea of starting my own animal rescue group had been with me for years before I finally embarked on this path. You might say it was destiny given my love of animals and relative unsuitability for a range of other pursuits that I'd attempted over the years. In the beginning, while I was volunteering for Oregon Humane Society, I met a woman named Sharon Harmon. She was the genius Executive Director who turned that organization into a juggernaut of humane societies. So, as a volunteer for OHS and then a person contemplating starting my own nonprofit rescue group, I could think of no one better than Sharon to consult about my idea. She probably doesn't even remember our conversation, but Sharon gave me the two pieces of advice that shaped my entire enterprise and that I haven't strayed from after all these years. She wisely suggested that I select a specific niche rather than trying to save every animal in the world. Then, further, she advised that I stay small and stick to my stated mission.

Ultimately, I chose to concentrate on pregnant dogs and cats and their offspring. I talk mostly in terms of dogs, but the truth was, I would rescue just about any species of animal that came my way as long as they were pregnant. I saw a need there because many shelters didn't have special facilities for neonates, nor did they have legions of foster volunteers who could be counted upon to care for these animals in their homes. I thought there was little sadder than a mom delivering her puppies in a cage or a kennel with barking dogs all around. That became my niche. And I was determined to bring in only pregnant animals and/or their litters from other shelters rather than from individuals. That's worked out well although I did take dogs from individuals once in a while when they had no other recourse available to them. I'm not perfect. And sometimes it was hard to say no.

In a best-case scenario at conventional shelters, if the pregnant dog herself was not euthanized, the puppies were often aborted by spaying the female while pregnant. The rationale was that there were already too many unwanted puppies, so why bring more into the world? I get it. This made sense to me in general and I wasn't a rabid right-to-lifer, but it seemed to me those puppies should have a chance at life. After all, this was Portland where there was a shortage of available dogs and puppies for adoption. In fact, a lot of shelters transported them here from other regions to save them from death row in kill shelters around the country.

The wisdom in keeping to Sharon's advice has been the secret sauce that has kept me from going crazy or burning out after the first couple of years in business. I freely admit that I can't save them all. But I like to think that I do my part and, together with all the other rescues and shelters, we *can* save them all.

Apparently, my chosen niche was a good one. Early on I found lots of private shelters and county dog control agencies willing to work with me. When they received a dog that turned out to be pregnant, they would call me and I would come and get her. She would then go to one of my foster homes (or stay in my home) where she could get acclimated and then have her puppies in a comfortable home environment.

What made my business model different was that I had recruited a special group of volunteer foster families who were devoted to caring for the moms and pups for extended periods of time. It takes a certain kind of person to open their home to an animal for months on end, transport her back and forth to vet appointments, and put up with a houseful of yipping, pooping puppies, as well as foot the bill for most of the expenses along the way.

In those early days, I was lucky to find a couple of veterinary clinics willing to spay and neuter the moms and the puppies pro bono. Operating on a shoestring budget, this allowed me to ensure 100% compliance with my own rule that all animals be altered prior to adoption. Giving these dogs a second chance came with the strict vow that this would be the end of the line. No additional puppies would be born to my animals. Period. My vets were heartily in favor of this rule and gave selflessly to my cause for several years. The way I found these big-hearted vets was to send out a simple postcard to all the local animal hospitals describing my organization and asking for their help. I can't thank those vets enough who responded to my little card and gave me a call.

I came to find out that the way most shelters made their money was by rapid turnover. That was clearly not possible when dealing with the raising of puppies. As mentioned, it takes several months to birth the puppies, wean them, raise them, and socialize them, and then have them all spayed and neutered prior to adoption. We didn't make a ton of money through adoption fees alone. As a small rescue group, we had no endowment and no one was making large donations. We had to come up with fundraisers of one kind and then another to fill that gap. A lot of local merchants were glad to sponsor us. Pet shops gave us dogfood and merchandise. We did dog washes, yard sales, provided boarding and walking, and did everything else that was legal and would provide money for the cause.

Just as an aside, most people think there must be some sort of parent-child relationship between the Humane Society of the United States (HSUS) or the American Society for the Protection of Children and Animals (ASPCA) and all the local humane societies in their communities. Not so. Each society is a separate 501(c)3 nonprofit organization. At the time I started up, there were few resources available to the little guy. We incorporated and followed all rules the big shelters did just so we could apply for funding to some of the mom-and-pop foundations who were interested in giving money to small rescues.

We issued a monthly newsletter that touted recent adoption success stories, gave general pet advice and information, and carried a wish-list of things we needed, such as cat litter, paper towels, etc. We also put out a plea for donations in every issue. Since the newsletter went out to a specialized audience of prior adopters, operators of pet businesses and other stakeholders, the resulting donations were spectacular. Animal people have a sincere desire to be of help and will do so monetarily even when they are unable to provide hands-on assistance. One hundred percent of our donations went to the animals. We had no administrative costs and no paid staff. Expenses such as pet food, equipment and postage were all strictly out-of-pocket. Our volunteers agreed up front to cover all their own costs except for veterinary care. The vets were separate and either donated their services or offered them at a discounted cost since we were a registered nonprofit. The newsletter gave endorsements for those vets and encouraged people to use them for their own pets. It was a mutually beneficial situation.

It wasn't long before we had built up a good reputation in the community. At the peak of our operation, we had more capacity than we were able to fill. I spent a fair amount of time on the phone coordinating the movement of pregnant animals and documenting all the known history of each one. We rescued both cats and dogs but decided at some point to scale back on the cats and concentrate on rescuing dogs. There were good homes to be found for the scraggliest, grouchiest, and sloppiest of dogs. That was the fun part. I took it as a personal challenge to find just the right home for each puppy and dog. Some of the less-than-cute mothers took a while to place but, eventually, they all found great homes.

Though Other Mothers was what could be called a limited admission shelter, that is, only a finite number of animals were accepted depending upon whether we had the financial and human resources to accommodate them, there was a steady stream of incoming moms looking for a port in the storm. Back in the boon years. just as soon as I got one litter spayed, neutered, vaccinated, and adopted, the phone rang, and I was bringing the next one in.

Typically, one of several partner shelters around the state would call me and ask if I had the capacity to take a new case. They would tell me what they knew of the animal, including how soon she was due to deliver her puppies, and I would make arrangements to go and pick her up as soon as possible. I always hated to say no because I knew these dogs were routinely euthanized - puppies and all - just because a shelter is such a poor habitat for a pregnant female.

This reluctance to say no has spurred me to cultivate a list of highly experienced foster families who can care for a mom and her pups in their home from early pregnancy through the time the puppies are weaned. People came to me from all sorts of backgrounds. Some were people like me who want to save an animal. Others were families anxious for their children to experience the miracle of birth. Yet others were empty nesters who just wanted some babies to cuddle. Regardless of their motives, the folks who became foster parents for Other Mothers either came in with an advanced background or soon gained an exceptional level of experience by raising their first litter with my guidance.

Without exception, the people who volunteered for foster duty were fully dedicated to their assignments. Not a single one has changed their mind mid-litter. This was saying a lot because I've had foster dogs bite people, destroy furniture, chew up designer handbags, and do all manner of damage out of fear and confusion. One brawny pit mom tore out a solid wood door to get to her pups being held temporarily in another room. These folks were committed to doing whatever needed to be done. I have my own theories about people who love animals this much. They were the same type of people who adopted our animals. And I've only had a few cases of buyer's remorse and just two bad checks in all the years I've been doing this. Even then, they were honest mistakes rather than any attempt to scam me or my organization. I've never considered myself much of a people person, but I will say that starting this group has shown me the best part of human nature.

Portland was such a special place at the inception of Other Mothers. The rescue dog had become our supreme being. We had rescue groups for deaf dogs, blind dogs, old dogs, dogs with various diseases and disorders and, of course, the ubiquitous breed rescues. The much-maligned pit bull breeds were especially embraced here in Doglandia. We even had an annual city event, Pitties on Parade, where pit bulls were dressed up in their pink Sunday best and invited to strut their stuff through downtown Portland.

Believe me when I tell you that rescued dogs feel grateful to their rescuers. Almost all the mothers that I have cared for exhibit the same incredible gratitude. The more wretched they are when arriving at my house, the harder they tried to please me. Once they'd had their puppies and recovered from the birthing process, they became these super tuned-in girls that seemed to have a sixth sense about how they could make me proud. My own two dogs, Scarlet and Sophie, were rescue dogs or, as we call them in the business, cases of foster failure. That is, they came to me for temporary help and never left.

Let me just say that I'm not generally a fan of little yappy dogs but somehow I have not one but two of these skittish little critters in my home. Scarlet and her "dog sister" Sophie both became mine because, simply, no one else wanted them. Scarlet become paraplegic in a tragic run-in with a German Shepherd. Sophie had no specific disabilities other than an unfortunate lack of noticeable intellect. But, again, she had the best of attitudes.

People always asked me about how I gained the confidence to start this thing and run it day in and day out. Part of the answer is simply age. I had enough life experience to say, what the hell, I'm going to do this. I'd been through the best and worst parts of a corporate career. I'd had my heart broken enough times to have developed a fairly thick skin. In other words, I've become a stubborn old broad who wasn't going to let anything stand in my way.

Once I took the step of buying my first home specifically for this purpose, I knew the rest of the plan would fall into place. I started hitting garage sales for dog crates and other equipment. I read up on all phases of animal husbandry. I consulted the experts for advice (such as Sharon Harmon at Oregon Humane). I networked the heck out of the animal community to find information and resources. I guess it just never occurred to people to question me. They believed in me simply because they could tell I wasn't going to take no for an answer.

I adapted two of my three bedrooms into a kind of canine maternity ward. It was an ongoing process. Next, I wanted to cover and enclose my back deck to make a comfy lounging area for my expectant moms. It would happen. Asking for money was not my strong suit but, even so, people were generous and found ways to help out when needed. It was just a matter of time until I'd come up with the money and know-how to further my deck project. If only all the world was made up of animal people.

Admittedly, a few of my neighbors and I didn't always see eye to eye about how I choose to utilize my property. I had one unpleasant old biddy to my south side who spent a fair amount of time looking through the slats in my fence just to see what was going on over here. Once, early on, she went so far as to call Animal Control on me with a wild (and completely untrue) story of a vicious pit bull running loose in the neighborhood. They came. They saw. They withdrew. What can I say? Some folks need to get a life of their own. To her credit, I have to add that this same woman was a confirmed "cat lady." She invited all the neighborhood cats into her home regularly to feed them delicacies and have them rest on her hearth. It was just the dogs that sent her over the edge. She hated dogs. And me, apparently.

Most of my neighbors seemed to put up with me admirably. Though I would have loved to hear what they said behind closed doors but, at least publicly and to my face, they didn't seem to mind my antics too much. I've been lucky that no one found a reason to try to sue me.

We had been a solid, well-oiled machine for over fifteen years by 2018. That was the first summer without dogs. I just couldn't locate any pregnant dogs to rescue. The reasons were twofold. First, other shelters were just as busy developing foster volunteers as I was. More and more often, an incoming pregnant female could be placed in their own foster network, and retained, rather than transferring her out to Other Mothers. Secondly, at least here in Portland, people were getting hip to spay/neuter and there were fewer unwanted litters out there in the community. It was a good result to years of preaching to the masses and I couldn't very well object to people heeding the message. Of course I missed the frequent pitter patter of little feet but, at the same time, I was happy to have been made largely obsolete. It meant that more dogs were being saved and that was why I started this enterprise to begin with. I knew I'd made a few enemies, but I'd also made some of the best friends a person could have – human and otherwise.

The evolving model for Other Mothers would necessitate bringing in dogs from kill shelters in other states and even other countries as well as those from local sources. I started to respond to this new reality by finding out how the bigger shelters were getting their dogs and by building relationships with organizations in other areas. Transportation was the biggest issue, but I was confident we could develop a small group of people who would travel back and forth between Portland and wherever. I imagined an army of retired animal lovers (myself included) who would be all too glad to respond to the call for a road trip when needed. The business was changing, certainly, but not going away for several more years.

Other Mothers has given me much in the way of enrichment, teaching me new skills, and allowing me to hobnob with some special animals and humans over the years that I'm not about to hang it up yet. There are still animals out there that need rescuing and I'm good at what I do. Why stop now?

DOING MY WORK

Although I tried to work quietly behind the scenes, partnering with various county agencies and private shelters, sometimes I needed to approach an individual owner about surrendering their pet. Early on, some of these fraught encounters went less than smoothly.

Let me just say that I am a large woman. I tend to intimidate people unless I remember to smile a lot. Then, when I smiled randomly and often, of course I looked like a big goon. I mostly wear yoga pants and men's tee shirts. These garments seemed to suit my special post-weight loss surgery body. My large purse is a crucial accoutrement with overladen zippers and bulging compartments. I don't go anywhere without one of my big purses. I have canoed the Amazon and walked the Great Wall with my purse clutched to my side. I have hiked the Appalachian Trail and ridden a gondola through the canals of Venice holding onto my bag. I have straddled the equator and made the Atlantic crossing with it. It contains vital makeup items, planning tools and various documents that allowed me to operate in the public eye. My purse was attached to me like a life preserver in a flood. I needed my purse. Calendar, lipstick, to-do lists. Without it, I was washed out, nothing. I needed my purse.

So, on one cool morning that passed for Spring in Oregon, I popped a couple of Vicodin for the sore back I had sustained lifting a pit bull mama in and out of the bathtub and clutched my bag more tightly. I was going in.

A broad smile bloomed across my face and I knocked at the door.

"Hello. I've come to help you with your cats." I paused and got right down to business. Tact was not in my repertoire. "May I take the pregnant female?"

The woman looked at me and the cat carrier I held at my side. She seemed to be considering her options. "Promise you won't kill her?"

I kept on smiling and shifted my purse. "No ma'am. We'll take good care of her. She and the kittens will go to good homes." I wasn't sure I sounded sincere enough. "I promise."

She probably thought I was nuts. I definitely thought she was. She let me take a pregnant calico that looked ready to give birth at any moment. I loaded the cat into the kennel and tried to assure the woman she was doing the right thing.

That was my schtick. It varied little from case to case. I would introduce myself and my mission and then I would make my ask. That was it. Working with other agencies was much easier than dealing with the public. The staff at these other shelters already knew who I was and why I was coming. All I needed to do was fill out their transfer paperwork and then load the animal into my car. Either way, dealing with people was by far the most challenging of my tasks as traveling doggy doula.

Fortunately, overcrowded brick and mortar shelters (and the occasional overwhelmed private citizen) trusted me enough to send their pregnant dogs and cats my way. I was able to find veterinarians, attorneys, media types and other professionals who were willing to donate their time and expertise. At the other end, when the babies had been birthed and were spayed or neutered and ready for their new homes, I was able to find more than enough qualified prospective adopters in and around Portland.

This was a unique city. Among other things, it is a City of Dogs. People travel with their dogs, dine with their dogs, shop with their dogs, and recreate with their dogs. They choose their dog's day care with the attention of a new mother choosing a pre-school. Dog park etiquette has reached the level of high culture here. It was the perfect city, perhaps the only city, where I could do what I did. And most of my clients were wonderful, if weird.

Having said that, I have encountered people who have shaken what little faith I had in human nature. I have come across people who shot cats for target practice and killed newborn puppies with a hammer. These people were aberrant freaks of nature, in my estimation, but they did exist. Even here. More common were the simply ignorant. They didn't think about having their dogs or cats neutered.

They never took them to the vet. And they didn't want them anymore when the animal developed bad habits, got fleas, or became pregnant. I knew I couldn't save them all. I've kept my mission limited on purpose so I can do one thing and do it well.

As I mentioned, I'm not a big people person under the best of circumstances. Fortunately, the interests and sheer desperation of my clients have made their messy situations easier to navigate. When I think I'm about to lose my mind, I am able to hang on until I can find a home for that last puppy. Then I could sometimes take time for renewal before the next animal came my way. Sometimes. There have been instances when one case overlaps the last, as with a recent German shepherd mom and a litter of unwanted chihuahuas. The shepherd mom, Heidi, nearly used up my last resource. She was a sweetheart, sound and gentle in every facet of her being. Except for one. She had a monster case of separation anxiety. When left alone, she would tear up the house in frustration. No one wanted her. I tried placing her as a service dog where she would be constantly accompanied, a country dog with acres on which to roam, and a companion to someone who purported to be an expert with the breed and its peculiarities. But my every effort was thwarted when Heidi would tear down a set of window blinds or break through a door to get out. And back she would come to me. I finally arrived at an uneasy compromise with a woman who felt the same sense of attachment to Heidi as I did and, though she couldn't keep her permanently, chose to take on the project of finding her next home herself. Sometimes a partial solution is better than none at all.

Heidi's puppies, and the chihuahuas, were easy to place. Everyone loves a puppy. While some of the moms were more challenging, it all eventually worked out okay. I managed to get everyone into a good home and then go on to the next case. As I approached my mid-sixties, more and more shelters had started to cultivate large staffs of volunteer foster parents that would raise their puppies, a fact that put a definite damper on my activities. But it was okay. I was slowing down too. If I could raise two or three litters a year, that was enough for me. I got my fur fix, the babies all got good homes, and I could concentrate on writing and traveling more.

To be sure, raising puppies was a labor-intensive enterprise. There was little time to look up and reflect, much less act on one's other interests in life. There were soiled papers to pick up and dispose of, puppy chow to dish up, little bodies to wash and calls to be made every hour of every day. It could only be a labor of love. There was no way operating as a serial puppy raiser can be anything else. Slowing down was not a terrible development and it came at the right time in my life. I was always able to come back to the dogs refreshed after a brief respite and was ready to jump into the fray once again.

As I was aging, I had developed some problems with my eyesight and hearing. And I was no longer able to walk the larger dogs without fear of being pulled off my feet. My depression was now and again rearing its ugly head as I worried about recurring health issues. The dogs kept me sane but, at the same time, it was more and more difficult to summon the mental and physical energies needed to take on each new case. I needed a major journey in order to refresh my day-to-day life. I chose Africa and I began planning for a safari trip to Kenya.

With a wriggling puppy in one arm and a tour book in the other, I was able to start thinking about something that had long been a dream of mine. Returning to the land from whence all life originated seemed like a fitting coda to my unlikely life. I'd gone through a lot of trauma over the years and experienced more than my share of what other people called blessings. I chose to concentrate on the latter. Life was finally good. I didn't want to miss that fact by dwelling on the things that were still wrong. My daughter struggled with a crippling anxiety. I had no partner in life. I was slated for eye surgery in a month. Still, there were good things. The animals still possessed their magic hold on me. I could think and I could write. I could travel. Now was the time to imagine one great big, ridiculous trip to Africa to refresh my soul and add to my book of memories. Well, not quite yet.

First I had to grapple with those health issues. At some point in the recent past, I'd noticed that my sight and my hearing, both on the right side, had started to deteriorate rapidly. After several tests and scans I learned that I had something called an acoustic neuroma between my auditory nerve and my brain stem. That explained my seemingly sudden hearing loss on the right side. It also explained my lack of balance when I walked or stood or tried to put my pants on, a problem I had previously ascribed to age and my generally poor physical condition. There was that. I also learned that I had a tear in the macula of my right eye. That *was* age-related. There seemed nothing to do about the neuroma, or tumor, except monitor its growth with a bi-annual MRI. I was stuck with the partial deafness, at least for the time being. As for my eye, there was a surgery to repair the macular hole and they were going to do it as soon as possible. Great. If there was one thing I wasn't looking forward to in life, it was having someone cut into my eyeball. Unfortunately, we don't always get what we want, and I was scheduled for surgery in a couple of weeks with the assurance that I would be heavily sedated and oblivious to what was happening up in my facial area.

In the meantime, I could only wait it out and try to be thankful for what I had. My eyesight would probably improve. Though she struggled with severe anxiety, my daughter Dinah was ready and willing to nurse me through the two-week period of relative immobility following surgery. And I would have the time I needed to recuperate before a planned trip to New York City that coming May. It would be okay. At least that's what I kept telling myself.

But I was, still and always, a depressive. I had to come up with a cogent way to impress upon Dinah that the challenges in my life due to depression were every bit as prominent as her own challenges with anxiety. I was feeling beaten down by her outbursts. She didn't understand why I wasn't better at helping her cope. She accused me of purposefully undermining her efforts when nothing could have been further from the truth. And that truth was that depression wasn't just a matter of sadness. It made me forgetful and unable to concentrate. It caused me to put off important tasks. It prevented me from applying myself meaningfully. These things were all the reasons that I self-immolated in my career after years of success. They were the reason the cat box would sit uncleaned sometimes and the living room unfurnished. I either didn't think of these things at all or, if I did think of them, they loomed impossible to tackle.

It was at this time that I wound up trying a new anti-depressant drug, Trintellix. I had been on the Prozac for over twenty years, off and on, and I doubted it was really doing me much good. I did notice some improvement when I added Abilify, a sort-of "helper" drug to the Prozac, a few years ago. The plan was to keep the Abilify and gradually taper off the Prozac while I was starting on the new drug. I felt like a pharmaceutical experiment in-progress.

And I had the talk with Dinah. She seemed to get the message and her outbursts and crying jags grew fewer, at least the ones she had previously blamed on my poor mothering. Perhaps the new drug was making me better. It was hard to tell. I planned to give it a fair trial and continued to take my psychiatrist's advice.

You could say, with some degree of understatement, that I had a few things going on in my life. There was also the overriding sense of having lived a period of my life under a cloud. I just woke up one day and I was sixty-five. My saddle and riding boots sat unused in the spare room. I had to face the fact that I would probably never get to ride a horse again. And, all kidding myself aside about meeting Mr. Right, I would probably be alone for the rest of my life. That, I felt I could come to terms with as stark as the reality loomed. Aloneness suited me. My only concern was how I would take care of myself once I became incapacitated by age. But it seemed a moot point. That might never even come to pass. I could die peacefully in my sleep or wind up in a suitable care facility when I needed one. The present took on a far more pressing importance. I probably had a lot of fairly good years left and I didn't want to waste them worrying. I couldn't let anything stand in the way of doing my primary work.

I had the eye surgery and continued to monitor the neuroma in my brain. My eyesight improved following the surgery, and I was confident I could deal with any eventuality brought on by my hearing loss. The doctors told me that most acoustic neuromas don't grow significantly over the years and most often don't require surgery or other treatments. If I had to find a bright side to that situation, it was that I was now allowed early boarding when I flew somewhere based on my hearing impairment.

TAKING CARE OF BUSINESS

Somewhere along the line, I'd received an email asking me if, as a member of Portland's "animal community," I would agree to appear in a commercial for a cat-related product. Of course I said yes. The day of the shoot kind of snuck up on me with everything else I had going on. But I showed up, wearing a bright blue sweater that I hoped would show up well on camera and more make-up than I usually wore.

There were eight of us there. We were ushered into the back of an industrial style building in Northwest Portland that I'd driven past a hundred times before but never noticed. A woman in a silk blouse and black pencil skirt welcomed us and told us the product being advertised was World's Greatest Cat Litter. I had seen it in the stores but never bought it. Too expensive. She said her name was Alex and we were to let her know if we had any questions as the day went on.

I already had a question. Why on earth had I gotten myself into this?! I was nervous about my appearance, my weight, my hair, my face. Alex showed us where we could find a soft drink and some snacks while we waited and then started ushering us one-by-one into another room to talk with the production assistant. When it was my turn, I found out I had chosen the appropriate shirt and didn't have to change into one of their garments. Thank goodness, as I was afraid they wouldn't have anything in my size. Next I went to makeup where they added a bunch of oily goo to my face – eye shadow, more mascara, rouge, and a fire engine red lipstick lined with brownish pencil. Good god, what did they think I was going to be selling?

Back in the green room, we waited and waited. Finally, all eight of us were led onto a stage of sorts. It was set up to look like a laboratory. A tall man in a lab coat and black horn-rimmed glasses sat at one end of a long table reading intently from a clipboard as we all filed in and took our seats in the order Alex had specified. Then, when instructed to begin, the tall man passed around a petri dish with cat litter in it and we were supposed to smell it and respond to the odor. One after another, we accepted the dish and held it to our noses. "It smells nice." "No urine smell here." "Surprisingly good." When it was my turn, I said, "I don't smell anything." They did this multiple times and finally told us we were done.

Alex led us back to the green room where we were allowed to collect our belongings and re-dress in our own clothes, if necessary, before leaving. As we exited the building, Alex handed us each a sealed envelope. Back in my car, I couldn't wait to tear it open. It held a collection of coupons for free World's Greatest Cat Litter. Awesome! I hadn't expected to receive anything of such value. At my house, cat litter was gold.

Nothing happened for a couple of months and then one day, on the Animal Planet, I saw my commercial. My line had made the final cut. There I was, big and bold in blue, sniffing the litter and proclaiming "I don't smell anything." I thought I looked huge and uncomfortable, which I guess I was. It was my finest hour.

But that wasn't the end of that particular adventure. Some months later, I was watching David Letterman and he was doing a bit showing people in bad jobs called "The Worst Gigs Ever" or something like that. Next thing I knew, my face was on the screen smelling that (supposedly) used cat litter. My appearance drew a laugh, I didn't know whether to be delighted or offended. Either way, I knew I had hit the big time.

Another time, I had gone to my local used book shop to get some paperbacks and the place was unexpectedly closed. I was told there was a student film crew inside shooting a horror movie. Obviously, I asked them if I could be in it. They dressed me up in a black cape with fur around the collar and hideous ghostly makeup and had me walk out from behind the shelves of books. I never found out whether the film was completed or what became of my performance but there it was. I had appeared in a movie.

On yet another occasion, I'd agreed to participate in a local Pet Fair. Not quite knowing what to expect, I suspected it was going to be a busy day and it was one of those days when I felt as if the cats were trying to kill me. This morning Benito wove his gristly old man's body between my feet while Shorty jumped out in front of me with a hiss. I nearly took a header over the coffee table. And it wasn't the first time. I'm certain one day to suffer the fate of the quintessential cat lady. I'll be found dead in my house and the cats will have been eating me. The little darlings.

But it was the day of the Pet Fair, and I was determined to arrive a little early to set up my booth, unfurl my signs and unload my puppies. I arrived with a grande café Misto from Starbucks (skinny, no foam) to sustain me. First thing, the donation box was prominently displayed, complete with a picture of a suitably irresistible day-old puppy and an appropriate quote from Dr. Martin Luther King, Jr: "*Our lives begin to end the day we become silent about things that matter.*" If that didn't pluck sufficiently at the heartstrings, of course there were the puppies themselves, seven bouncing babies in all colors.

People wandered by, shopping for dog supplies. Many stopped to chat, donating a dollar or five to experience some sweet puppy breath in their faces. Then my neighbor for the day's event arrived. Fortunately, it was not another rescue group competing with me for good puppy homes. But, god help me, it was a self-proclaimed animal communicator. And she chose to take advantage of our proximity to communicate with me.

First, she went into her schtick about how she had always had the ability to talk with animals. She told me she had a special calling and she lived to bridge the gap between people and their pets. Mostly she seemed to be telling people what their animals were saying – rather than the other way around. I thought it would have been more helpful to tell animals what their people were saying. It would solve many more problems. "Bailey, either you start peeing outside or you'll be looking for a new place to park your Kong toy." That would have been a hell of a lot more helpful than telling the hapless owner, "Bailey pees on the carpet because she's stressed about the new baby." Of course, if this communicator could have delivered the owner's message to the dog, the average mutt would probably realize we were bluffing. But we'll never know because the hotline worked one way and one way only.

In any case, Sylvie, as her name turned out to be, tried reading my puppies. It turned out they didn't have a lot on their minds. Who knew. But she went on to describe for me some of her more triumphant readings. This killed about an hour. It was almost noon and traffic was slowing down at the pet fair. Three puppies had been adopted thus far and there were four remaining. I cleaned up the occasional "oopsy" and continued listening to Sylvie's amazing feats of communication. Neither of us was drawing much attention at the moment.

Finally, a guy in worn jeans and a red hoodie walked in and pulled me aside.

"Will you waive the adoption fee and give me a puppy for free?" he wanted to know. "I don't have any money. I can't work because I'm disabled. Bipolar. Sometimes I get really, really mad. And I have, you know, a *record* so no one will hire me."

Uh oh. Did I risk incurring his ire by questioning whether he could offer a good home to a puppy at this point in his life? As it turns out, that was my only option and I took it, plunging right ahead into, for me, uncharted territory.

"Actually," I began, "I would be afraid all the yelling and stomping might scare a little puppy. And how could you afford it if you had to take him to the vet?"

He took several seconds to digest my words and, surprisingly, he agreed. He may have been subject to fits of rage, but he wasn't unreasonable. He said he wouldn't want his own puppy to fear him. Then he surprised me further by starting to cry. Big tears welled up in this 40-something year old man's eyes. He heaved a sigh and wiped his eyes with the sleeve of his hoodie. I wound up sitting him down and letting him hold a puppy.

He was sobbing loudly, and Sylvie was trying to tell me what the puppy had to say about the situation. The event manager, Brian, came over and asked if everything was alright. Back in the planning stages, I had gotten the creepy feeling that Brian had a crush on me. He was tall and thin with tattoos of vegetables inexplicably displayed up and down his lanky arms. Oh, and I out-aged him by perhaps 30 years. I assured him that things couldn't be peachier, and he wandered away with a winsome smile. I turned back to my visitor and saw that the puppy was indeed lifting his mood. He was smiling and still crying at the same time. This guy reminded me a little bit of myself. Eventually, he gave the brave pup a kiss on her head and returned her to her littermates. He hung around for a little while longer, then said good-bye and wandered off.

Then, in fairly rapid succession, two families came in, passed muster, and adopted puppies. And then there were two left. Sylvie shared some gossip that she had heard from a Maltese over in aisle 4. Turned out either Sylvie or the Maltese had a really lurid way with a story and soon the afternoon came to a successful end. I went through a reverse of my set-up process, rolling up the signs, putting away the full-ish donation box and crating the remaining puppies for the ride home. There were some good prospective adopters. I had picked the best of them to take home my little darlings. We made money. I was able to find homes for most of the puppies. Everyone was happy. The event was a success.

At the end of the day, I had only the two puppies left to cart home. They were tired after the day's activities and slept all evening. Tired puppies were indeed good puppies. No messes. Nothing broken or knocked over. It was an easy night.

I settled in to watch some news. At about 8 o'clock, a man called looking to adopt a pair of puppies together. I talked with him for a little while and declared him worthy.

He came out the next morning to fill out the contracts and pick up his puppies. I had always depended on my gut to make decisions about adoption applicants and I had a good track record. Though I knew I could be judgmental, this was a situation where it paid off. When I was working, I was good at hiring the right person for the right job. In my current incarnation, I felt capable of sizing up prospective owners quickly and with a minimum of fuss. This was one skill that was directly transferable from the insurance business to animal rescue. There weren't many. And that was probably a good thing as, aside from the people I met, worked with, and helped, I didn't really enjoy the world of life insurance.

I did miss an aspect of the work for a while when I first retired. But that was mainly just the familiarity and sense of belonging and, given the terms of my separation, overall I was relieved to be away from the business. Looking back now, as traumatic as it was, I can see that my breakdown allowed me to move on to something much more fulfilling. I guess that's the gift of hindsight. When it comes to business meetings and office politics, give me a bunch of diarrhetic puppies and a freezer full of cats anytime.

MY GIRLS

I acquired Scarlet four summers ago from a woman in the military who was being deployed and couldn't take her puppy with her. The woman was referred to me by her vet and had reached out by phone to see if I could help her. Every day seemed to find me in the middle of other peoples' dilemmas and, fortunately, I was often able to deliver a solution.

Foresight is a trait sadly lacking in far too many pet owners. The sad fact is that I often come by animals that are not successfully planned into moves, new jobs, and marriages. People just don't think. They are overtaken by the cuteness of that sloe-eyed little puppy or kitten and can't resist bringing them home. Then comes the passage of time and, along with it, the relocation, the promotion, or the new spouse and – whoops! – the pet, no longer small and cute, doesn't fit into the plan. But I guess that's partially why I'm here, to facilitate a new home for the unwanted "old" pet. And, sometimes, when conditions align just right – or terribly wrong – I wind up being permanently on the receiving end. Such was the case with Scarlet.

I arrived on the doorstep just as the owner and her little daughter were returning from a walk with the puppy. The small pup was happily romping along at the end of a pink leash. The woman opened her door and invited me in.

The apartment was in a state of transition, the floor littered with half-filled moving boxes and piles of personal belongings. Along the living room wall sat rows of books, unhung artwork, and décor items. She still had most items out and useable but ready to box up at a moment's notice. The staging was familiar. I could tell this was a woman used to frequent moves.

"She's a nice little dog," she began. She picked up a pillow from the couch and began nervously picking at the fringe. I could see she was fighting back tears. Her daughter, a little blond girl about nine or ten years old, sat on an adjacent chair and watched her mother struggle.

I knew her story all too well. I had come to a place in my own mind where I didn't personally blame people too much for their mistakes. I had to. Otherwise, I would have grown to be a terrible self-hating misanthrope. Things happen. We can't always foresee the future.

"We love her so much," she tried again. "But we just can't keep her." The little dog, unperturbed, wagged her tail and plopped down on the cool linoleum floor. "Can you take her?"

She was a six-month old teacup Chihuahua with short reddish-brown fur and perfectly round caramel-colored eyes.

There was no question that I could and would take her. She would be easily adoptable. And, in the meantime, I would enjoy having her. After a short briefing on her mealtime habits and other likes and dislikes, the woman handed over the small bundle wrapped in a blanket, and I stood to leave. The young girl had left the room, presumably to avoid having to say goodbye. I found myself wondering who would be taking care of *her* in her mother's absence.

Formerly called Laura, I soon realized this dog needed a name as epic and dramatic as her personality. And she was a real Scarlet O'Hara. I could see her sweeping through the halls of a grand plantation, overseeing the staff and special events with grand flourishes of crinoline and lace. Scarlet was also, as fitting her diva nature, a bit on the bossy side and I found she didn't get on well with my neurotic German Shepherd, Maggie. I established a gateway feature at the point where my living room and kitchen gave way to the hall that led to the back of the house. Maggie's domain was to be the front area where she could go outside via the kitchen door. And Scarlet, who could be carried outside, lived in the back bedrooms. That way, I could spend an equal amount of time with each of them, but they wouldn't have to cross paths unnecessarily.

One particularly hectic day, I burst out of my bedroom on some now-forgotten errand and didn't notice that the hallway gate was open. Scarlet had burst out with me and had run right into Maggie who was lying in the living room. The ensuing fray lasted only a few seconds but one bite was all it took to forever damage Scarlet's little spine. She lay on her side on the floor panting, gravely injured and in shock. There was no blood. I gathered her up and rushed her to my vet but there was nothing that he could do. He said she would never have a normal life. He recommended that she be put down. Since she wasn't in pain and because of my profound sense of guilt in what had occurred, I decided to take her home and care for her in the off chance that she might improve.

This was the kind of accident I would have been all too tempted to blame on another owner so I had to take full responsibility for what I had done that allowed this to happen. Primarily, I had to face the fact that Maggie, who I had acquired from an overwhelmed breeder, was not safe around other animals and probably not around humans either. After some past incidents and near-misses, I had been putting off the decision for months. But the sudden clarity hit me like a ton of bricks. It was just a matter of time before she got a chance to attack a child or some unsuspecting adult visitor. I couldn't control her. And she was a nervous, unhappy dog. I was forced to make the sad decision to euthanize her. It was one of the few occasions I'd ever had to make this decision, but I was sure it was for the best in this case. Nonetheless, it was hard on me and I won't elaborate on all the tears I shed. My emphasis ultimately had to be to concentrate on helping little Scarlet.

The plan was always to have her spayed and place her in a new adoptive home along with the next batch of puppies I raised. I never thought that I would keep her myself. It was what we called in the pet-rescue business a case of "foster failure." You take in a dog and get them all ready to be adopted and then – blammy! – you fall in love. It doesn't occur often, thank goodness, but when it does, there's nothing that could make you rehome that dog. And, old hand that I was, I didn't see this creeping up on me. It just kind of happened.

I had found a canine rehabilitation clinic that was willing to take her on pro bono since my rescue operation was a registered 501(c)3 nonprofit. Scarlet spent months undergoing water therapy and acupressure to strengthen her muscles. Ultimately, there was nothing that could be done for her compromised spinal cord so she was never going to learn to walk by herself again. She got to the point where she could pull herself along with her forelegs and move about just as quickly and nimbly as an able-bodied dog. I was so heartened to see her attitude in all of this that I knew I'd done the right thing in choosing to work with her. Unlike a human, who might have sat around feeling sorry and defeated, Scarlet put herself in the middle of all household activity in short order. She was a can-do sort of gal.

We got her a wheelchair cart. There wasn't a dog version small enough for her so we adapted a cat cart for her use. It had a suspension system to support her rear quarters and big round wheels in back. She took to it right away. After a couple of early crashes when she took a corner too short, she was soon an expert user. Although she still scooted around on her own inside the house, the cart was the perfect vehicle for walks outside in the sunshine. She loved it.

Her only other unresolved issue was her bowel and bladder function over which she still had no control. I got into the habit of manually stimulating her to go a couple of times daily and that was usually enough to keep her tidy around the house. It was the least I could do for such a champ.

Then came the day I realized that she was my dog. I had actually found an adopter willing to take on a special needs animal. The woman and I got together a couple of times and I'd shown her how to take care of Scarlet's daily needs. She met Scarlet and liked her. She took her home. I don't remember thinking anything might be amiss until she called me a few days later.

"I just don't have the time for her," she said. "Work is taking up most of my time and when I get home at night, well, I just don't think I can keep up with this." It was clearly more than a matter of time. Scarlet's disability was a heartbreaker for her. Given this dog's awesome and upbeat personality, I couldn't stand the thought of someone feeling sorry for her.

"No problem," I replied. I always let people know that I would take back any animal for any reason. It was the only way to keep my charges from winding up in a shelter – which is where most of them came from to begin with – and to ensure the success of my mission.

"I'm so sorry." She sounded like she thought she was letting me down.

"Really. It's not a problem." I could feel my own enthusiasm growing. Uh oh. She was going to be my dog. There would be no more tentative placements, no more crossing my fingers that it would work out. She was going to be my dog. I knew it as surely as I knew anything.

Her already-forceful personality had continued to evolve. She was the first to prick up her ears and grab at any offered treat. She greedily eyed any other dog or cat who might be enjoying a snack of their own within her purview. And, as follows, she'd developed a bit of a weight issue. Already top-heavy with huge chest and shoulder muscles from pulling and wheeling herself around, she continued to gain weight. While my other Chihuahua, Sophie, weighed in at a svelte four pounds, Scarlet had ballooned to 9 pounds and sported a double chin. She was still a beautiful little lady. If she were a person, one would be tempted to say, "She has such a pretty face."

Scarlet eventually mellowed some in her middle years and was accepting of the other dog moms and puppies that found their way into my home. She seemed to know they were only temporary and would be leaving one day soon while she stayed on as queen of the castle. Perhaps she planned it that way all along.

Sophie came to me in another way entirely. She was one of my shelter moms. Picked up as a pregnant stray, the staff of a nearby county dog control agency called me to help. She was a great little mom. She had four teeny-tiny puppies in my bedroom and took care of all of them without problems.

When it was time for the adoptions, the little puppies found homes readily but no one seemed to want the bow-legged mom with the wonky eye and propensity for pointless hysteria.

Sophie was not the shiniest egg in the nest. She hurled herself hither and yon like a piece of errant popcorn, not knowing where she would land or if she would land on her feet. She barked in a high yodeling tone and for no good reason. She feared the cats' gaze. Fortunately, she fell into line behind the alpha dog, Scarlet, and worshipped the ground Scarlet walked on. Or, rather, the ground that she scooted on, for Scarlet was still pulling herself along by her front legs, taking corners at great speed and dexterity when a treat demanded her attention.

At four pounds, Sophie was petite, even for a chihuahua. Although scrawny might be a better definition of her appearance. The thought of her running around loose as a stray scared me to death. She didn't have the sense God gave a flea. That being said, though she was neither intelligent nor lovely to look at, she did possess a certain down-home charm.

She came to me in late pregnancy and gave birth to four pups that were adopted immediately as soon as they were ready. But nobody fell for Sophie. I wound up keeping her. That was the story of my life when it came to running an animal rescue group. The ones no one wanted. The ones with insurmountable challenges. The ones with poor temperaments or buggy eyes.

I once hosted a pregnant girl called Snoopy who came to me angry and stayed that way through the first few months of our acquaintance. She was an oversize chihuahua mix with spiky hair and big feet. I can't count the number of bites I suffered just trying to groom and feed her. When it came time to find a home for her, I knew it was going to be a tough sell. She barked at absolutely everyone and tried her best to bite them. She finally got to the point where she thought of my home as her territory and was all the more aggressive trying to protect it. I took her out many times to show her on neutral ground, took her to parking lots and parks and to many people's houses who had no other pets. But barking and lunging were her bailiwick, and no one was willing to take a chance on her. I kept trying until I came across an unfortunate woman who had lost her children to Child Protective Services because she had been homeless. Finally in an apartment and lonely, she met Snoopy, was promptly bitten, and decided to take a chance on her anyway. For a month, I called her every night to check in and ask if she wanted to return Snoopy yet. But she hung in there and they finally became the best of friends. The last time I talked with this woman, she had been given her children back and Snoopy was even great with them. Go figure. The point was, there was a home out there for some of the most unlikely pets and I was patient, even dogged, about seeking those homes out.

Sophie was one who still couldn't find her special person no matter how hard I tried. And try I did for at least six months before coming to the conclusion that she was meant to be my dog. And I loved her scatterbrained little personality right from the start. When she barked, which was often and for no discernable reason, she sounded like she was singing a bad song, all high-pitched and atonal. She was clumsy, stared off into space, jumped blindly in the hope of landing someplace near my lap. She appeared to eat invisible morsels off the floor and then dislodge them from her mouth with urgent gesticulations. Her behavior was so bizarre that I thought for a time that she must be in the throes of seizures. Eventually my vet was able to rule that out. Her senses were working fine thank you very much, she was just a bit of an eccentric. I liked to think we had that in common.

Sophie was not only the smallest little wisp of a dog, but she was largely bald due to a chronic case of nervous scratching. I'd spent thousands of dollars on her in vet bills, medications, behavioral nostrums, grooming products and special diets before coming to that simple answer. She just wanted to scratch herself. It was like a person who cracks his knuckles or bites his nails. She never scratched so hard as to draw blood like some of the dogs and cats I'd seen with really bad skin allergies. She just scratched long enough to keep certain areas of her mousy little body mostly hairless. Her chest. The backs of her hind legs. (Her thighs?) And the front of her forelegs.

To add to her unfortunate appearance, she had the ugliest big, splayed-out feet of any dog I'd ever seen. The vet was of the opinion that she may have inherited her hyper-extended chicken feet as a result of poor breeding or, more likely, developed in that way due to lack of good nutrition as a puppy. He also thought she would be more likely to develop arthritis as an older dog because of this. There was something else she and I had in common. The arthritis, not the ugly feet.

For all of her oddities, she was still the best little trooper ever. She had an infectious can-do attitude and was an all-around good egg. Next to my other dog, Scarlett's, smugness and imperious attitude, Sophie's Holly Go Lightly optimism was a real treat. She was up for anything except interactions with the cats. The cats terrified Sophie and she would scream bloody murder if one of them so much as looked her way. Even the gentle Blancmange sent her running and yodeling. In time, Scarlett toned down her haughtiness a bit when poor Sophie would go running to her in fear of getting the evil eye from one of the cats.

What I've learned from Sophie is this: Everyone is different. And that's really okay. It apparently makes some people uncomfortable or stand-offish. Which is why she's never found her special person. And very likely why I've never found my special person either. Thank goodness we have each other. I wouldn't rehome her now for the world. She, like Scarlett with her lack of bowel and bladder control and her nippy ways, belongs with me. They're really the best two dogs in the whole world and I wouldn't change a thing about either one of them.

THE PARENTS

Klaus called. I'm sure I wasn't the only person in the world who has a brother who didn't like driving in unfamiliar places. Or in traffic. Or in rain. He wanted me to take him fishing the next day. Okay. I didn't mind. It gave us a chance to visit. Oh no. Wait. Tomorrow I had to take my mom grocery shopping. Fishing would have to wait until the following day.

I had to say that Klaus's absurdist worldview was about the only thing that kept me sane for as long as I did remain sane. If you expect, as he seemed to, for everything to be impossibly convoluted, you'll never be surprised by life's twists and turns. He always seemed to cope so well. I tried to emulate his matter-of-factness in the face of challenging times. But shopping with my mom presented a whole new level of distress.

My parents – god help me! – were both in their mid-nineties and were relying more and more on me to drive them around and do things at home for them. I didn't mind helping them, it was just that they lived a good hour and a half away and routinely had me come over to change a lightbulb or put new batteries in my dad's hearing aids. It took a lot of time.

I guess, at their age, I should have been glad they were still alive. But it killed me to see my mom dithering around at the grocery store, unable to remember what she came for or where to find it in a place she'd been to a hundred times before. Or worse, she'd forget the name of a common item. And repeat herself again and again and again. And my dad? Forget about it. He was almost completely deaf and got irritated when he couldn't hear something. The TV was always on at full blast. They seemed to have a channel that showed nothing but old "In the Heat of the Night" reruns.

I drove down to take mom shopping and could hear the TV blaring as I walked up the driveway.

"Come in, the door's open." I wondered how she always knew I was there before I knocked. "Come in, come in, come in."

I went in and inquired about how they were and what they'd been doing. Okay and nothing were the usual answers. What else was to be expected when they had no friends, no hobbies, no real interests? This time my mom said she'd fallen down the night before and hadn't been able to get up. They had to call 911 so they could get her back on her feet. Besides a faint bruise on one side of her face, she wasn't injured.

"You know, I couldn't get her up," my dad said. "I don't know if I'm getting weaker or if she's getting heavier." This is his idea of a joke.

I laugh.

"What?" he says. "What did you say? I didn't hear you." And then to my mom, "Goddammit, turn that TV down. You can't hear anything in here."

"I didn't say anything, dad."

"Okay, fine. You can't be bothered to repeat yourself. That's just fine. I don't need to know what you said."

"I didn't say anything, dad" I repeat, much more loudly this time.

"What? Oh, never mind." He changed course. "Dammit, what do I have to do to get a hot cup of coffee around here?"

"I'll get it," I shouted, taking his cup and going into the kitchen. There were still groceries on the counter from the last time we shopped almost a week ago. I put them away, tossing out some ruined lunchmeat and a dozen eggs.

It occurred to me for the hundredth time that they shouldn't be living alone in their home any longer. The time had come for them to move into some sort of assisted living facility. But they wouldn't hear of it. They didn't want to spend the money. Klaus always said they would be the first people ever to find a way to actually take it with them. I didn't doubt it.

As uncommitted as they always were about everything else in life – child rearing, family, any kind of social life – they were always passionate about their money. And they'd made a ton of it throughout their long lives by raking it in and never spending a dime. They owned their house outright. There were no investments. It just went into a savings account month after month, year after year, until now they had several hundred thousand dollars sitting in the bank. And they wouldn't hear of paying rent at a nice retirement home. Or going out to eat. Or paying a housekeeper. To each their own, I suppose.

It only bothered me because I would have liked to see them get some enjoyment out of life. And the money could have made their lives easier, made their lives better. But no. They'd be subsisting on a diet of off-brand Vienna sausages and dented cans of beans for the rest of their lives. And, truth be told, maybe they were onto something. They hadn't outlived everyone else by doing all the wrong things. Who knows what's been keeping them going all this time? Klaus thought it was probably all the preservatives in the food they ate.

I loaded my mom's walker into the car trunk while she told my dad four times not to go outside while we were gone.

"What?"

"Don't go outside. You might fall down."

"Oh, alright, goddammit, I won't go outside."

"And don't lock the door. We won't be able to get back in." Of course she had a house key but was always afraid the door would jam or somehow she'd be locked out. "Don't lock the door."

"What?"

"Don't lock the door." She put on her coat and picked up her purse. "And don't go outside. Do you hear me?"

"Yes, I hear you. I'll see you when you come back. Drive carefully."

And off we went. She had a shopping list as long as my arm. She needed to go by the eye doctor. And to the insurance office. And she needed some of that special (read cheap) canned coffee from BiMart. It was going to be a long day.

Somehow, we got it all done and returned home before dark. I asked them if they wanted me to stay and make some dinner but they did not, saying they weren't hungry yet. I put away the grocery bags in the little caddy my mom kept behind the laundry room door. And I set off for my place, an hour and a half away, thinking about going fishing the next day with Klaus. I didn't even like to fish. I usually just sat in the car and read while Klaus smoked cigarettes and sat on the bank with his fishing pole.

Dinah called me on my cell. "Where are you?" she wanted to know.

"I'm just leaving Albany. I'll be home within a couple of hours. Will you be there?"

"No," she says. "Frank is taking me out to eat. Then we're going to his house. It smells too bad to stay here. And Pilkington threw up again. I think he has cancer. Will you look at him when you get here?"

"Okay, I'll look at him, but I don't think … Oh, never mind. Yes, I'll take a look at him. Just be careful out there, okay?"

"Mother, I'm almost forty!" Her usual answer to any sign of concern.

"I'm well aware of how old you are. Just have a good time, okay? Where are you going to eat?"

"Geez, I don't know. Leave me alone." She sighed theatrically. "Just out, that's all. To a restaurant. Okay?"

"Okay. Fine. Bye" Afraid to say any more, I hung up and enjoyed the drive. Alone.

THE CATS

Did the phone have to start ringing every time I was elbow-deep in a dog bath? It never failed. Did I mention I only have two hands?

"Hello?" I tried to keep the impatience out of my voice while I blew a strand of hair up out of my face.

It was Klaus.

"Well, the world's going to hell in a handbasket." There was no one like Klaus to state the obvious. "Trump is saying he's the greatest president since Lincoln."

"Yes, I know," I answered. "Promises made. Promises kept. Yada yada yada."

What would I do without Klaus? I read somewhere that your relationships with your siblings are the longest ones you'll have in your life, longer even than those with your parents or your children. I guess I lucked out there. Klaus was the one person who always accepted me the way I was.

"I'm going into town tomorrow. Do you want to meet for pancakes?" he asked, as if for the first time.

This had become our weekly ritual. Meeting at IHOP for a short stack to discuss his garden and whatever insane events were taking place in *my* life at the time. It was amazing what all could be said about a garden. What was doing well. What was struggling. How many tomatoes he'd picked that morning. If I was lucky, he would bring me a couple of zucchinis or some fresh string beans in a brown paper sack. And I would bring him news of my latest animals, sometimes with photos, or, less often, a piece of writing I'd had published.

These meetings meant a lot to me. They were just about the only adult conversations I ever had on a regular basis besides my strained interactions with Dinah and the occasional lunch date with one of my writing buddies.

Klaus always knew when I was struggling. And that was most all of the time. In spite of the latest in antidepressant drugs I was taking, life tended to be difficult for me. My visits with Klaus never failed to bring me back up.

"My spuds are just about ready. The plants are starting to die back." He added, "That's how you know they're ready."

"Oh yeah?" He had told me this before, but I didn't mind hearing it again. "And how are the leeks coming along?"

And so it went. After an hour passed, we would pay up and leave. Until the following week.

There were also our fishing trips where Klaus would fish and I would sit in the car and read. And our trips to the

Indian casino where we would meet for lunch and then each go off to play our respective games, video poker for him and video keno for myself.

I savored these times as if they were already in the past. I knew that one day they would be and that lent them a melancholy quality. Where would I be without Klaus?

One chilly Spring afternoon after the animal chores were done, I went to my room and turned up the thermostat. The dry baseboard heat wafted over me in waves, doing my soul good. Scarlet and Sophie had sat up in their beds, looking at me with their ears pricked up and their huge saucer eyes limpid in the low light. Sophie was wearing a red gingham frock that said "Mommie's Bestie" across the back. Scarlett wasn't wearing anything. She had shimmied out of her dress as soon as I'd left the room earlier, as she normally did.

Looking beyond them out the window, the lilac bush was starting to green up. I could see the tiny buds beginning to swell. I loved the way it smelled every May, sweet and cloying like an old lady's cologne. Another month or so should do it, I thought.

The cats began to file in for the evening. The first two were Pilkington and Blancmange. Pilkington was named for the street I was on when I first realized that he was going to be my cat. He was a stout flame point longhair with a perpetual judgmental scowl and a myopic gaze. He tended to keep his own counsel. His sibling, Blancmange, was named for the French dessert I had recently encountered on a trip to

Europe. He was an elegant seal point, gentle and lovely. Together they decorated my living room sofa with white fur and the occasional hacked-up hairball.

In addition to the brothers, I had Benito and Shorty. Every morning, when I opened my bedroom door to the world, all four cats would stream in for some one-on-one with their person. In came Benito, the old man, a white-and-gray tabby with enormous, bulbous green eyes. For all his long life, he had been haughty and bellicose, very un-catlike. I suspect he was a despot in another lifetime, perhaps ruling over a kingdom of submissive little mice who cowered at his every move. I know *I* did. Benito, or "Neets," was as likely to bite me as to say meow. I had arrived at a grudging respect for his unnatural churlishness. He was a character.

Behind Neets came Shorty, the only cat in the world good-tempered enough to put up with Benito. Shorty was another tabby, sleek and fat, and a friend to all creatures. She would sweetly groom Benito for as long as he would stand for it and then lie close to him as if to assure him that he had one friend in the world. Shorty was a good egg. She loved all the puppies and kittens that came through my house like some kind of feline Mary Poppins, leading them around and teaching them by perfect example the tricks of the trade, namely begging and looking cute. At the same time, Shorty was our alpha cat and not above clouting the others when her rules were not followed.

Shorty heaved her plump body in my direction, letting out a plaintive meow. Blancmange scooted over to give her a little more room on the bed, licking at his tail nervously. If only my family members were more like cats. Independent. Self-possessed. But now I was making myself sound crazy, right? The crazy cat lady. That's me, I guess. There's no getting around it. I was probably ill-prepared for any other role in life, so tainted was my upbringing as a nomadic army brat. There were many things I never learned. And in many ways, I couldn't be like a regular person, couldn't empathize, couldn't relate. I could only observe and try to blend in with them, with the normals. Maybe I was a bit like a cat myself.

I had just had a lavish catio built so the cats could access the great outdoors safely from a back bedroom window. I'd furnished it with ferns and ornamental grasses in pots and installed a carpet of lush sod for their pleasure. Only Pilkington showed any interest in the new cat porch, choosing to perch on the windowsill and look out rather than commit to entering. It's okay, I told myself, they'll learn to love it.

These four cats, all products of foster failure, served as the Greek chorus of my life. They sat staunchly, expressing their pointed opinions of whatever happened within my purview. Now, they were strategically arrayed across my bed, jockeying for position and sparing occasional disdainful glances at the dogs. And while the dogs were slavishly devoted, as is the wont of dogs, the cats chose to gift me with each conversation, each interaction. They looked at me impassively from behind their Harlequin masks and spoke in their measured collective voice to my every move and mood. I couldn't have functioned without them.

OUT OF THE ORDINARY

Though I dealt most often with cats and dogs, every once in a while somebody would throw me a curve ball. Last year, Multnomah County called me with a couple of month-old piglets. They had been found along the side of a road and brought into the shelter. Shelter staff didn't know what to do with them, so they called me. Interestingly, in looking back, I didn't think twice about taking them. I must have been craving a sense of novelty in my life. I named them Maxwell and Alexandra and set them up in my bedroom in a kiddy wading pool full of straw. No sir, nothing odd about this situation.

It turned out they were smarter and cleaner than any of my puppies. They took to following me around the house. They were adept at peeing on newspaper and eating their pig chow out of little china bowls. The thing was, these were farm pigs, not cute little potbelly pigs. These guys would grow up to weight six hundred pounds each. And they had almost-human blue eyes. I would catch them looking at me surreptitiously from behind their long lashes. It was as if they were sizing me up, considering my motives. I was definitely being tested. What on earth was I going to do with them? Being a meat-eater myself, I felt a bit hypocritical about not wanting them to end up as bacon. But, honestly, knowing them the way I did, there was no way I was going to turn them over to a conventional farm. I started my online search for a sanctuary. In the end, I was lucky enough to find a place that was willing to take them, a sort-of retirement home for farm animals. I was able to visit them later, at six months, and they still remembered me. I could tell by the way they looked at me from behind those long eyelashes of theirs. All in all, it was a positive experience. Things usually turned out okay when I said "yes."

Another time, I picked up a new dog named Cookie from a local shelter, a pit bull/beagle mix that was all skin and bones. And pregnant. Everything went normally until the pups were about a month old and the foster mom called me to say she thought two of the pups were "swimmers." This is a condition she'd read about on the internet. The term is used to describe a puppy that paddles his legs much like a turtle but is unable to stand. A puppy should be standing and walking by three weeks of age. As a result of weak muscles in the rear limbs, swimmer puppies are generally unable to stand at the normal age.

The foster mom turned out to be right. The puppies were eventually diagnosed with cerebellar hypoplasia, a disorder where the cerebellum of the brain has not fully formed. There are various causes including bacterial or viral infections, but it can also be caused by poisoning, injury or malnutrition. In any event, we watched them grow into otherwise normal, healthy pups. Their only problem was the inability to walk or run in a straight line.

Not surprisingly, no one wanted to adopt these two girls. I was at my wit's end when my veterinarian mentioned she had a colleague working in neurology at the local vet school. She was interested in examining the puppies with this rare disease. Eventually she would adopt them out to a couple of her students who understood what the disorder was all about and who would promise to love these little girls just the same. It sounded like the solution to my problem. Then, apparently, the colleague went overseas and couldn't be reached for first two weeks and then two months and the next thing you know it's six months later and I was still caring for these puppies. I'd been pinning all hope on the possibility that the plan would still work out. I never euthanized animals short of a life-and-death reason but now I was starting to wonder what I would ever do with these helpless little ones. I tried to remain hopeful.

Their mother, Cookie, continued to pee in the house and jump up on me causing bruises all over my legs and arms. Other than that, she was a dear. I still didn't have a home for her either. I couldn't remember a time when I had to hold onto animals for so long before they were adopted. I didn't mind admitting that I was tired and ready for a break. Even when using foster volunteers for the day-to-day care, I had to check in with them to give advice, provide supplies, facilitate vet trips, etc. And always I hoped they wouldn't change their mind mid-assignment and insist on bringing the animals back to me prematurely. There were small problems along the way but things tended to work out eventually. But, as I said, I'd never had to keep a dog and some of her litter for so long.

Finally, some good news. The foster mom called me after many months and asked if I still had the little swimmers. She wanted one for herself and agreed to adopt the other one out of her home. Great news, I thought. And then while I was still basking in my good fortune, another woman whom I had been in touch with recently called me about Cookie. She had to go on a week-long business trip but, if I would hold the dog for her, she promised to give her a good home. Yes! It was another instance of things turning out okay.

On the same day, with all of the above resolved, I got a call from a woman who I'd previously assisted with an unwanted litter. Now her brother-in-law had the same problem – a female that had *accidentally* gotten pregnant. She said they couldn't afford the puppies and would I take them? My respite was over. I told her I would and I hoped that they would at least allow the puppies to stay with mom until they were weaned. I risked betraying a bit of snarkiness here, but I had to think that some people have apparently never heard of spay/neuter. The nonplussed woman said she would call me back when they were ready to let go of the puppies in a month or so.

A few weeks went by and I started to wonder when I would be picking up the puppies. I did get a call finally from the woman, but it was to tell me that the pups had been seized by the police. Great. Knowing there are always two sides to a story, I tracked down the puppies where they had been taken and called the director of that shelter to see if they would consider ceding them over to me. It turned out the pups were confiscated due to malnourishment and sores on their feet from walking around in their own waste. The deputy who seized the puppies later told me that they had also been exposed to meth in the home. Nevertheless, I was assured they would be well cared for, not euthanized and, eventually, all neutered prior to being adopted. It was time for me to butt out. I decided to leave well enough alone.

Since I'd promised to call back the sister-in-law of the errant owner to let her know the outcome of my communication with the authorities, I needed to do that in a somewhat tactful manner. I didn't want to piss her off because she would almost certainly call on me again in the future with another puppy "emergency." I called her and left out the part about her brother-in-law's meth habit, just letting her know that the puppies would be in good hands. Some people were, to put it bluntly, ignorant. And, to be honest, tact was still not my strong suit. In any case, I believed the woman's intentions were good. She wanted the best for the dogs. I wasn't sure the same could be said of the brother-in-law.

When I wound up not getting that litter, I called up my contact in another county shelter to see if they had any pregnant moms or bottle puppies for me. I had everything set up to receive. I even had newspapers down on the floor already.

So, ask and ye shall receive. The next day I was on my way out of town to pick up a pregnant pit mix. The dog control facility at that particular location was a rundown industrial-looking building across from the county jail. They employed inmates as volunteers to help care for the animals. It was kind of depressing but seemed like a great assignment if you had to be in jail. My contact, Ruthie, came out from behind the counter and welcomed me.

"Let's get the paperwork done and then we'll get her out, okay?" She was a short, stout woman with a bowl-shaped haircut. "There's just one thing..."

Uh oh. There was always just one thing.

"She has some socialization issues," Ruthie went on. "We've had a couple of incidents with her."

I had learned this euphemism to mean she was a mankiller.

Undeterred, I patted and rubbed the monster's broad anvil-shaped head when she was produced a few minutes later. She smiled, as only pit bulls can do, and drooled in my lap. I knew we were going to be fine. I'd have to warn the foster mom that she might be temperamental. I couldn't help but think about what a good idea it was that I'd developed a waiver form for these good people to agree to when they signed on with me. But I did have a good feeling about this dog. She was going to be okay. I knew I could trust my gut in these matters.

In my mind, she was already called Ruby. I loaded her into the front seat of my Honda since she was too big for the kennel I'd brought. She sat and looked out the window all the way to her new home. I wasn't mauled and the foster mom loved her right away.

I'd either been incredibly lucky or perhaps I had really good common sense when it came to dog matters. I couldn't say I'd never been bitten but I had never been seriously injured. And I'd never been the subject of litigation. Moreover, my track record for keeping dogs in their new homes was superior to most other shelters and rescue groups in the area. This was true in spite of the fact that I didn't require references or home visits prior to adoptions as many of the shelters were starting to do. Again, I just relied on my gut to tell me when a person was an acceptable adopter. It wasn't difficult. You knew by the kinds of questions they asked. You knew by what they said had happened to the last dog they owned. Mostly you knew by the look in their eyes when they held that sweet puppy and told me they wanted to take him home. I'm not gloating or being self-congratulatory. It's just that I continued to surprise myself that I'd gotten something so right over the years. My former corporate life be damned. This was something that I was good at.

BABY BUSINESS

In my mind, my little house is called the Wayward Wind Ranch. It's from the old Patsy Cline record that talks about the wayward wind being a restless wind that yearns to wander. That's the way I feel. Ever since I was a kid, I've been a peripatetic soul. Then, by necessity. And, now, by choice. Even though I don't move around as often I once did, I prefer to travel and then return to my home base to recharge between trips. Home is my haven.

I think all those years while I was working at Ensign Insurance, I was growing stagnant through lack of movement. I had become generally ineffectual, frustrated and impotent. Until I found Other Mothers as an outlet for my passion for animals, I was blocked up inside, not connected to anything that moved me. My juices were not flowing. Or perhaps it was just the misfiring of all those wrong pharmaceuticals while they searched for the right combination of drugs. Nothing was clicking.

Whatever the case, once I bought my small Southwest Portland cottage and filled it with animals, I had found a groove. I no longer had to work to prove myself. I was free to retire and spend my life as a doggy doula, rescuing pregnant animals from death row and assisting them, along with their offspring, toward adoption and the good life.

One April morning, when the crocuses were blooming in my front yard and the grass, as usual, needed mowing, a little bug-eyed cocker spaniel named Dotty went into labor in my bedroom. She was using a child's wading pool as her whelping pen and with each contraction she braced herself against pictures of little green froggies. The pool was just the right size and shape to contain the puppies and to allow for Dotty's ease of access. I had a heat lamp set up to provide extra warmth, its source diffused by aluminum foil with holes poked in it This protected Dotty from accidental contact and would protect the puppies' eyes from bright light. The floor of the pool was covered with multiple layers of newspaper to ensure a sterile field. I had a blue laundry basket at the ready to receive each newborn pup, lined with a heating pad covered by a towel. The other accoutrements of my trade included a big plastic bag for soiled newspaper and other garbage, a stack of clean towels, a pair of sterilized blunt-end scissors in a sealed plastic bag, dental floss, a food scale denominated in ounces and a pediatric rubber bulb syringe to clear little airways.

Brave Dotty had been pacing and panting for a good six hours and she finally plopped down on her side to start pushing out the first puppy. The first one always took the longest as it served to fully open the cervix. After four strong contractions, the amniotic sac emerged. Dotty tore open the sac and stimulated the pup to breathe without any assistance from me. Then she waited for me to cut and tie the umbilical cord before proceeding to deliver the placenta. I picked up the puppy head-down and placed it in the warmed laundry basket to give Dotty the room she needed to repeat the process. After about three hours with breaks in the action to nurse her new puppies, she had given birth to six little oblong bodies about five inches in length and all brown-and-white pied like their mom. There were two males and four females. I marked down each one's vital statistics in turn: time of birth, sex, weight, color, and markings. I then placed a numbered band around each little neck.

The puppies were all nursing well and I had accounted for all the placentas. Dotty ate the first two of them and left the rest for me to clean up. Good dog. She climbed out of the pool after another hour to eat a light meal and have a big drink of water. I went to get an iced tea and returned to watch their progress. It had been an easy birth, and everything went according to plan. I was feeling proud and happy to have assisted.

By evening time, I was comfortably ensconced with the new family. Me, watching a home remodeling show on TV, the new puppies sucking enthusiastically and Dotty attentive to her motherly duties, licking and nuzzling each pup in turn. Scarlett and Sophie waited in the living room like a couple of anxious aunties. The cats were sequestered on the covered patio to be out of the way and enjoy a little fresh air.

It never gets old, this birthing thing. I continued to marvel at each new life and each new mother who seemed to know the territory so well even when it was her first time. Once in a while, a new mom would panic or become distraught but that's why I was there. Only once in thirteen years had I needed to bundle one off to the vet for an emergency cesarean section. And stillborn puppies or abnormalities were mercifully rare. Overwhelmingly, Mother Nature puts on an awesome show.

On one particularly cold and drizzly Portland day, I found myself in the midst of a new crisis with Other Mothers. I had lost my supporting veterinarians and had no means of free spay and neuter surgeries for my puppies and my moms. With this turn of events, I had to come up with a way of staying in business that didn't involve my going broke. My mission clearly included an end to these animals' reproductive functions. I couldn't bring myself to adopt them out unaltered, even with a stringent spay/neuter contract in place. I had to be 100% sure that none of my puppies and kittens would have little ones of their own.

In the past I hit on the bright idea of sending out a postcard to all the local veterinary hospitals asking for donation of professional services in return for my recommending their clinics to all the new adopters. This approach brought a series of three vets that had lasted me for all of ten years in business. But there were no takers this time around and I faltered, suffering an entire year of no babies because I couldn't afford to have them altered on my own dime.

Then I hit upon a new approach. I could make use of low-cost spay-neuter coupons available online for some local vets and, at the same time, increase my adoption fee from $100 to $400. The increase was more in line with what other shelters were charging in the area so it didn't seem entirely outrageous. With that change in emphasis, the business took off again with a bang.

That January brought me a litter of three adorable chihuahua puppies whose owner had offered them up on the NextDoor app free for the taking. I convinced her that they would be better off with me, well cared for, spayed and neutered, vaccinated, etc., etc., before being adopted out to carefully screened new homes. She apparently saw the wisdom in my plea and decided to give them up to me once they reached eight weeks of age. The litter was three quarters chihuahua and one quarter Pomeranian which gave them a tiny size and a nice fluffy coat. I moved them into my bedroom in a puppy pen alongside Scarlet and Sophie, the two grand dames of the Wayward Wind Ranch.

The original owner was a curious specimen. A disabled middle-aged mother struggling to get by, she had inherited a female chihuahua when her mother passed away, a female which had quickly gotten pregnant by her intact male. She seemed to have no compunction about this unrestrained population boon and, like many less well-to-do clients I had served, didn't fully appreciate the benefits of spay/neuter.

Yes, it was a costly procedure but it was far less costly in the long run than raising litter after litter of puppies. Once I had taken possession of the three current pups, and before I could again raise the option with her of having her females spayed at my expense, she let me know another female had gotten out and been impregnated by her male. That meant I would be lucky enough to get those puppies too but missed the point of limiting all the wanton procreation.

Aside from my frustration with the owner, the pups were a delight. Small and crafty, they fit right into my current population of canine misfits, learning to beg and climb onto my bed with the best of them. I clipped their little nails and gave them baths, vaccinated and dewormed them, and planned for them to be altered when they reached the requisite two pounds. At that time, I bundled them off to the local cut-rate veterinary hospital for their procedures and made plans to host an adoption event. PetSmart had a string of upscale supply stores called Unleashed where I had an ongoing relationship with one of the store managers. I brought all my puppies to him for adoption and, in return, he donated a ton of surplus pet food and equipment. The upside for him of hosting these events was that, for every puppy adopted, the new owner invariably spent from a little to a lot of money buying supplies in his store. It was another of those symbiotic relationships upon which my business was built and flourished.

In the meantime, while I waited for the pups to mature sufficiently that I could put my plan for them into action, they continued to live in my room in a four-foot diameter puppy pen. When I wasn't cleaning up after them, I was playing with them or cuddling them. Now nine weeks old, they were still babies after all.

One morning I awoke and headed for the coffee pot to prepare the morning brew when I ran into my daughter Dinah in the hallway. "Morning," I said.

"Morning," she answered back.

That was our usual a.m. exchange.

"What the hell is *that*?" It looks like a rat!" I saw something lying in a dark corner that caught my eye as being repulsive and out of the ordinary. "Is that a *rat*?!"

"Calm down mom. It's a cat toy. You need to have your eyes checked."

"It looks like a rat to me."

"Mom, look at it." She sighed. "It's wearing a little vest."

"Oh, I guess you're right."

So began the morning. Once I'd gotten my coffee, and my senses properly honed, I was able to face the day. Sometimes it was better to do the dirty work of puppy maintenance before I had my coffee but that morning I needed it in order to glove up and get going.

The pups were looking especially cute. One of the three apparently had more of the Pomeranian genes than the chihuahua. He was a little brown furball and appeared twice as large as his sisters due to all the fluff. He had a curly tail and floppy ears. The middle sister was a soft dilute chocolate color with a beautiful, little, white-marked face. Then there was the tiny girl. She was impossibly petite with a long, graceful neck and a bit of an underbite. All three were real characters and I loved to watch them frolic and play.

I had scheduled their spay/neuters for the following week and set up an adoption event for two weeks out. Everything was ready. I knew I wouldn't have any trouble placing this trio. They were simply adorable. No two ways about it. Unfortunately, the cuteness factor didn't ameliorate the mess or the smell. Cleaning up after puppies is no one's idea of a good time.

After I had everything tidied up, I decided to go and give them all a bath. I piled up three fluffy towels, a measuring cup for rinsing and a gentle shampoo on the kitchen counter by the sink. Then I went to get the first of the three pups. It was the male, and he was a good sport. No major scrabbling around or complaining. Then I did the tiny runt. She cringed and whimpered a little but hung in there okay. Lastly, I plucked out the middle pup and held her gently under a stream of warm water. You would have thought I was holding her under hot lava by the way she shrieked. What a diva. But I got them all bathed and dried and their tiny toenails clipped. They were exhausted and fell into a heap asleep. After I'd cleaned up the wet mess in the kitchen, I was ready to join them.

Somehow I had missed the weather forecast and snow was starting to fall. Whether it would be a light dusting or the Snow-magedon promised by the local network news was yet to be seen. All I knew was that they do a lousy job of plowing and salting in Portland and it doesn't take much to make the whole place a slippery mess. Back in Iowa, it would snow up over the windowsills but once you'd gotten yourself dug out, and your car uncovered, you could navigate the roads without undue danger. What I remembered too was that, in Iowa, if you *did* get stuck in a ditch, someone would come along and tow you out in short order. Here in Portland, that would never happen. It's not that they're unfriendly here, it just that they are more respectful and less involved with the doings of their neighbors. You tell me which is better.

In any event, I went to the store yesterday to pick up a few odds and ends and encountered an end-of-the-world fervor in the WinCo parking lot and in the aisles. People were buying generators, space heaters and cans of beans by the case. They were evidently prepping for the "Big One." I got my cat litter and a stack of Lean Cuisine dinners and got the heck out of Dodge.

If the worst-case scenario developed, I guess I would be S.O.L. but I somehow didn't think it would come to that. Maybe we'd have a couple of snow and ice days and then we'd warm up and be back to normal. I just hoped I would be able to get the puppies to the vet for their surgeries. If I was unable to venture out on the designated day, that would delay the adoption event until at least the next weekend. I didn't want to say the puppies weren't still cute, but I was anxious to turn them into money and get it in the bank. One never knew when the next pregnant mama would come along and need a helping hand.

With the snow upon us, one of my foster volunteers called. She found herself in possession of a little pig that needed a home. While I thought her husband was unusually laid back about all the stray animals she collected, he'd apparently had his fill with the arrival of this pig. It was a little red-haired Kunekune pig named Penny and just as cute as it could be. Since this was my second foray into the realm of pig-keeping, I wasn't unduly put out at the prospect of finding a sanctuary where she could live without fear of being made into bacon. I emailed all around the state and finally found a farm animal sanctuary that said they could take her.

The weather cleared and arrangements were made. I picked up Penny on the appointed day to drive her to her new home in a place called Jacksonville, Oregon. On the way, Penny and I decided to take a little side trip to the casino on I-5 just North of Medford. It was fortunately a pleasant enough afternoon in early February that Penny was comfortable relaxing in the car while I went in to try my luck. It was a good five-hour drive from Portland so I didn't want to stay longer than necessary at any stop along the way. Nonetheless, the lure of keno was strong and I ventured inside for thirty to forty minutes of gaming and to enjoy a complementary beverage.

Not coincidentally, I had made a decision to go road tripping to Reno in May after a cruise planned for April. I was in fair financial shape at the moment. All I had to do was hold onto the four thousand dollars extra I had in my bank account until I could execute both trips. I knew it wouldn't be easy – money surely had a way of slipping through my fingers – but I was determined to do some traveling this year come hell or high water. Perhaps Klaus would join me for the Reno trip. He was currently forty-sixty in favor of going thanks to a recent win at our local tribal casino.

Once I'd found the sanctuary, I pulled into the lot in a rooster tail of dust and parked next to a big red barn. The proprietor, Sandy, came out to meet us and offered to show me around the farm. It was a fairly thriving enterprise with all manner of farm animals living happily and free from the meat trade. I couldn't help but feel a little bit hypocritical after my breakfast that morning of bacon and eggs. Just the same, it was somewhat idyllic to see and hear stories of the animals living there.

Once I'd assured myself that Penny was in good hands, I started back up the I-5 toward Portland eager to get home and check the slew of phone messages that had surely accumulated in my absence. Each would be another adventure waiting to take wing.

DINAH

This is not about Dinah, who is beautiful, clever, and complex. What follows is about me, my grappling with her demons which are my own as well. Dinah is a bit of an enigma, a woman of heart and integrity, but also a woman stalked by worries that are dire and close at hand. These are the issues of which I speak here, and these issues only, because, if truth be told, I blame myself for their plaguing her. Who else is to blame but a mother?

Dinah had struggled with anxiety for most of her adult life. It reared its head by keeping her from finishing things she started and overreacting to things going on around her. A child that had been kind, intelligent and curious about the world turned into a fearful, peevish recluse. As a mother, it killed me to witness the changes in her.

So traumatized had I been by my own mother's neutral response to my childhood problems that I wound up going full speed ahead in the opposite direction. That is, I internalized Dinah's anxiety and took it all on myself. I felt that I should have been able to fix her. And instead of thinking about empowering her to manage her own life decisions, I tried to control every aspect of her life. And I was in a perpetual impotent rage.

I wanted to swoop in and save her from herself. It didn't work when she got into trouble as a kid and it sure as hell didn't work now that she was an adult. I was driving myself to distraction trying. I was never taught to be resilient. And now I felt the walls closing in from all directions.

At eighteen, after dropping out of high school, I had talked Dinah into going to Portland State University. Her college career was prolonged and unsatisfying. She finally quit for good after seven or eight years, with no degree and owing a small fortune in student loans. Throughout her twenties and thirties, her work life was a similar slow-burning catastrophe consisting of numerous menial jobs of short duration. I didn't care about the jobs as much as I did about school. I wanted desperately for her to finish her education. I wanted her to have choices that I did not have. But it wasn't to be.

By this time, she was back home living with me and working part-time as a server in an Indian restaurant. She refused counseling or medication. Her anxiety had grown worse until I was sure that, if I didn't give her a place to live, she would be literally homeless. I came to accept the reality of her limitations grudgingly and only after many years of the misguided belief that she would wake up one day and be "normal."

Of course, I blamed myself. I blamed her absent father. I blamed *her*. Ultimately, there was no one left to blame. The situation was the way it was. I felt that it was better to house her and provide for her so long as she was productive to the best of her abilities and could contribute to the household each month. But the hell of it was, she resented me for acting like a mother and wanting more for her. She couldn't come to terms with the fact that she and I would never be just housemates. I would always be the mom and she always the daughter. If she felt strangled, what I felt was sorrow for all the lost potential.

And, if I was being honest, I did feel cheated. Not only would I never see her graduate from college, but I believed that I would never have a nice son-in-law or precious grandchildren to spoil. Her relationships with men were like everything else, ill-advised and incomplete. Dinah had not married and was reconciled to the fact that she would never have children. The only reason she had been able to keep her current job for a couple of years was, as she explained, because it was a dark setting where no one could see her clearly. As it was, there were some days when it was all she could do to get ready for work without a total meltdown. One morning, Dinah was crying in her room, bemoaning the fact that she was having so much trouble whipping herself into shape for work. I'd learned to be quiet. Any attempt I made to encourage or cajole her was met with anger and rejection. In short, it only made matters worse. I was holed up in my own room, trying not to involve myself in the train wreck of her day.

"Mom," I heard her call out. "Mom! Can you take me to work? I don't have enough money on my card to take an Uber. And the bus, well, you know I can't take the bus."

"Okay, I can take you. What time?"

"I don't know what time. Don't ask me. It puts too much pressure on me to be ready on time. I can feel you watching the clock and judging me." She trailed off, talking more to herself than to me.

"Well, how am I supposed to know when we're leaving?" I asked.

"I'll tell you when I'm ready. Just leave me alone."

"Okay. Fine." There went *my* whole afternoon. What could I do? If left to her own devices, she would fail to succeed in the simplest of routines. Between my own depression and her dad's myriad list of alleged mental health diagnoses – depression, anxiety, OCD, PTSD – I was afraid Dinah was doomed. How could I possibly distance myself from a mother's responsibility? Should I even try?

"I have to open my window," she said.

"But it's wintertime. It's cold outside." I knew as I said it that I was fighting a losing battle. I put on a robe over my clothes. "Just be sure to close it when we leave."

"I will, I will." She slammed her door. "What am I going to wear? Oh my god, I don't have anything clean to wear. My last pair of black pants has cat hair all over them. *Everything* has cat hair all over it."

Okay, here we go again. The animals. It always came down to the animals. They were ruining her life. I admit, with a base population now of four cats and two dogs, plus whatever foster animals I happened to be housing at any time, there may have been some hair. And some odor. But Dinah was hypersensitive. She had refused to make cookies once recently for fear that an errant cat hair would bake itself in with the chocolate chips and nuts. She wouldn't bring anyone to the house because she said she was too embarrassed by the smell. She thought the dogs were always peeing on her stuff. She thought all the animals were suffering from obscure diseases that she read about online. Or worse, that they had emotional issues due to overcrowding.

What was a person to do? I admit I was not the most scrupulous of housekeepers, but it wasn't really that bad. Honest. I emptied the cats' litter boxes every day or two and cleaned up the barfed-up hairballs every time I saw one. And the dogs? They were spoiled rotten. It didn't help that little Scarlet had a spinal injury and couldn't control her bladder and bowels. I had to express her manually a couple of times a day and sometimes a little piece of poop got left in her wake as she scurried from room to room. Was that so bad? I thought I was doing my due diligence by ripping out all the carpet and having vinyl flooring installed throughout the house. I did my best. Honest. But it was never good enough.

What I failed to recognize most of the time during that period was that Dinah, under all the neuroses, was a wise and kind person. She was smart as a whip in spite of her limited educational experience. She was a true friend to the ragtag band of misfits that orbited around her. When she would admit me into her world, she was caring and loving. I didn't learn until she was an adult that she had a lot of resentment built up toward me from her childhood. She didn't believe that I loved her enough. What a cruel joke, after my own dark childhood.

We struggled together to get along under the same roof. As a depressive myself, her presence probably wasn't healthy for me. She had too many dramatic ups and downs. But there was no way I could separate myself from them. As vociferous as her claims to the contrary, she needed me. Of that I was convinced. Only once in a great while did we arrive on the same wavelength where I could peer into her soul and see the little girl I had raised.

For a long time, I was so hung up on what was normal and what was not normal that I didn't realize my good fortune. Although I would still be overjoyed if Dinah went off on her own feeling strong and independent, at this point I was starting to see the gift inherent in having her there with me. She didn't do much work around the house and the two of us had little in common in the way of pastimes, but I loved seeing her face in the morning and having her around to talk with. I was learning that there was a person in there beyond her limitations, a person who was kind and thoughtful, a person who was funny and smart, a person who had dreams like I did and who would see a way through her challenges to reach them.

When Dinah first came back to me at age thirty-five, unemployed, hopeless, and riddled with her peculiar set of anxieties, I could only think of it as a failure. A failure to thrive. And I had been through blaming myself and blaming her father and blaming her. Now none of it mattered. Could I have been a better mother? Of course. But I always did the best that I could and I always loved my daughter more than anything else in the whole world. Early on, I would try to nag her, cajole her, reason with her, do anything to try to get her to do what was "normal" like go to school and finish her degree, get a serious boyfriend, look for a good job and make some money, etc. etc. etc. I now realized these were the same expectations that were placed on me over the years of my young adulthood. I met some of them in time and with varying degrees of success but none of them brought me much happiness. All that I ever wanted or needed was to be loved and accepted for who I was. And here I was appearing to withhold that prize from my own daughter.

I wanted Dinah to want to please me enough that she would do those things that I thought she should do. I told myself I wanted her to be able to benefit from my mistakes. But it was more than that. I wanted her to be one of my successes, even if it were just on the surface like my own marriage, career, etc. God help me, I was treating her like she was only there to reflect on me, either positively or negatively, but not as a person in her own right. Of course, I saw all this now that I'd had a chance to live with her ups and downs these past few years. I saw it all but I didn't think I had thus far succeeded in letting her know these things. She needed to know that all I wanted was for her to find happiness to the best of her own, personal potential. It was what everyone wanted for their kids. Maybe she knew it, intuited it, but I was horrible at conveying these things to her.

Here I went blaming things on my bad childhood again, but the truth was, I was never nurtured. I never learned to accept love or show love, to open myself up where I could be hurt, or to give someone a chance to reject me. As a fat person, and a person with some of my own personal idiosyncrasies, I knew a lot of rejection. No one really chose me. I wheedled my way into a career, a marriage, other pursuits. No one has ever pulled me into their world and welcomed me there. Mostly, I just existed on the fringes. Maybe this was some of what Dinah felt but I didn't know for sure. She grew up a beautiful, accomplished and very *wanted* girl. All I knew for sure was that I had failed miserably to let her know that she was remarkable in my eyes. I hoped it was not too late for her to discover this.

I myself have never suffered from a fear of failure. It's what I did all of the time. But Dinah was different. She feared failure so much that she was frozen with indecision. She sabotaged herself rather than making an honest effort at anything. Take school. She was plenty intelligent to have racked up all kinds of academic accolades and to now be enjoying a successful, professional career doing anything in the whole, wide world. But her fear held her back, made completing each single course a Sisyphean endeavor. She would rather drop out or simply not show up than to embrace the challenge and give it her best. I didn't know why this was. True, I always did expect a lot from Dinah in school. I knew she was gifted. But I didn't make a big deal out of an occasional bad grade. Kids get bored. Kids get distracted. I understood that. Why was she afraid to fail? Why did she lack the confidence in herself that everyone else, myself included, felt for her? I guess the bottom line has become for her that if you don't try anything then you can't fail. And that, of course, was wrong. In fact, it was the only way to guarantee constant failure. Nothing ventured, nothing gained, right?

I heard somewhere recently that success was continuing to fail over and over again without losing one's enthusiasm. I get that. Success was inevitable if you kept trying. You didn't have to tell me that. I was a walking billboard for tenacity in the face of long odds. What had I done to this kid? Why was she so afraid? Or was this just me placing myself in the middle of her world again? Still?

Could it be that Dinah's fear was the result of simple bad chemistry in her brain? And if she happened onto the right combination of therapy and medication, would she, like her mother, start seeing a light at the end of the tunnel? Maybe this was what I should stress with her, the importance of seeking professional help for her problems. Or maybe I should just butt out. Who's to say?

Through all the problems, all the missed opportunities and all the failed communications, I hoped to hell that Dinah knew deep down how much I loved her. I could say it. I could know it was so. But I was a bloody failure at convincing her of this simple truth. Or at least I had been so far. Maybe the cards have been shuffled and redealt now that I can see a little more clearly for myself. Maybe I could succeed at this one important thing. I worked at this dilemma like a sculptor shaping clay, smoothing, gouging, reworking until the piece was beautiful and complete. But there I was again putting myself in the role of savior. And, truth be told, I can love her but I couldn't save her. She had to save herself. But I could believe in her. That I could do.

There it was. My own truths. My own crippling struggles. Dinah was my angel and, together, our mental illnesses were being allowed to define us. There had to be more to us than our common clinical maladies. There had to be more in the world than looking at ourselves with this jaundiced eye. I believed there was more and that Dinah, not I, held the key. I was the past and she the future.

KITTEN SEASON

It was kitten season, that Spring surge in cat reproductivity that annually strains the resources of every animal shelter and rescue group in existence. Among those of us in the business, kitten season was a joke. The truth was it was kitten season all year round.

On one rainy morning, I was called out to extricate a batch of newborns from under a house. It seemed like a routine call. It turned out to be a muddy worksite where a new house was being built. One of the workers told me he was the one who called. He said he hadn't actually seen the kittens, but he knew they were there. On the basis of the feeble little meows coming from openings in the foundation, he had pulled the plug on construction until the kittens could be located and hoisted to safety.

Here I was with a crew of impatient men and a concerned contractor. He took me around to each corner of the building in progress, kneeling down and saying, "Listen. Do you hear anything?" Nothing. I must have crawled on my hands and knees at least five times around the house before I heard something. Maybe.

The question shifted then to how we could get them out. I stood by while the three men assessed their relative sizes to identify the smallest guy. It sure wasn't me. They were all too polite to say so. Once identified, he was the lucky stiff who got to squeeze himself into the mucky crawlspace with a big police-style flashlight tucked under one arm in order to search the close quarters for signs of life. The rest of us waited aboveground like relatives in a maternity ward until a hand and arm came up out of the darkness with a tiny gray kitten at the end of it.

I scooped the kitten carefully from his palm and placed it in the crate I had brought. In a few minutes another appeared. And then another. All together we collected a trio of week-old kittens with no mom anywhere in sight. They were weak and hungry and, from their looks, didn't have a lot of time to waste.

After bringing the little ones home and setting them on the road to recovery, I called the contractor back a few days later to let him know all three kittens had survived. The guy continued to call me weekly for status reports until each baby had gone to a new loving home. He must have mentioned five times that he wasn't a cat person. We wound up naming the little male kittens Cliff, Kenny, and Jeff after the contractor and two of his workers.

I continued to be glad this guy took time out of his day to investigate those muffled noises and then get on his phone to look up who to call. I wished everyone exhibited the simple kindness this busy man showed. He could as easily have just ignored the sounds and continued on with his work.

You can never tell by looking which people are going to be animal lovers and which are not. Sometimes a burly construction worker will take the time to save three helpless kittens. His call restored my faith in human nature. It was easy to judge people when you're in this line of work. This was a lesson for me.

I wouldn't dwell on all the uncaring and downright abusive people I have met since starting to rescue animals. They were not worth the time it took to remember them. It was the softies who mattered, the folks who understood that every life was important, that no creature was too small or too raggedy to rate our empathy.

True, I have come across my share of downright nutty animal people. The nuttiest among them might not be people who I would care to spend a lot of personal time with, but they are alright in my eyes. They are my people. In fact, I've more or less taken it for granted that these people – all right, I'll admit it, they're almost all women – will come my way. And, truth be told, I was one of them.

One such woman, by the name of Debra Dearborn, came my way via a phone call one chilly March morning. She had a batch of kittens, all related but none of them littermates, that she didn't know what to do with.

"Where did they come from?" I ventured. I was sure there must be a story here someplace.

She went on to explain to me how she had a colony of cats on her property that continued to reproduce until she was currently unable to keep up with the demand for new homes. I gave her my lecture on TNR (Trap-Neuter-Release) and asked her if she would be open to that.

"Oh yes," she enthused. "That would be perfect. But what am I going to do with all the little ones?"

"I can take them," I heard myself saying, wondering just how many there were and what kind of shape they were in. "Can you bring them to me? Or maybe we could meet somewhere?"

We arranged to get together at a far Southeast Portland Denny's restaurant that we both knew. She met me there with a large cardboard box in the back seat of her minivan with a large book on top of it to keep the contents from bursting forth. I carefully wrangled it, book and all, into my Honda. Then we chatted and I arranged to go out to her property the following week to start trapping cats.

It wasn't until I got home that I was able to peek inside the box. There were eight kittens, all white, and about six weeks old. They took over my house. They were the most daring and most curious among all kittens, forever climbing my drapes, getting into drawers, and jumping from the top of my refrigerator. They developed beautiful color point coats of both long and short hair varieties. Two of them particularly won me over and I wound up keeping them, naming them Pilkington and Blancmange. The rest found their forever homes and my house was restored to relative normalcy.

Since then, I could count on getting a call from Debra Dearborn once every Summer with a delivery of white kittens. We trapped and trapped and trapped but somehow never got the population explosion entirely under control no matter what we did. I grew accustomed to the yearly onslaught of fluffy white kittens and came to anticipate their arrival with a certain degree of restrained enthusiasm.

One year she did not call. Good, I thought, we'd finally captured the last of the fertile females. Then, again the following year, she failed to contact me. I was feeling as though my efforts were finally not in vain, congratulating myself on the dent I'd been able to make the in burgeoning kitten population of the far East Portland exurbs. My experiences with Ms. Dearborn faded into the background and I went on with the business of rehabbing kittens that came my way from first one source and then another.

At some point after five years or so of no contact, I happened to be chatting with another cat rescuer at a meeting of a citizens' advisory committee to which I belonged when I was told the story of an ongoing rain of kittens from a single source on the East side.

It sounded so much like my past with Debra Dearborn that I had to ask. "What is this woman's name?"

"Her name is Dearborn. Debra Dearborn," the woman answered with curiosity evident in her voice. "Why do you ask? Do you know her?"

I proceeded to tell her the tale of my own experience and how it had come to an abrupt end five summers ago.

"That's so funny," she replied. "The first time this woman called me, she told me her houseful of kittens had just shredded the phone number of the rescue she used to work with. "It had to be you."

"Yes, it was me, I agreed." We had a little laugh over the coincidence and went on with the meeting in progress.

I didn't think any more about it until one day the phone rang as I was coming in the door with a load of groceries. It was Debra Dearborn. We had the same conversation we'd had multiple times in the past. I agreed to meet her at Denny's.

It wasn't until later that day that it occurred to me the woman from the animal services meeting had given Debra my phone number again, passing her on like the proverbial hot potato. Now I can take a joke as well as anyone but this seemed to me a little mean-spirited. I vowed to get even. And though I never did, I'll long remember the lull in activity that temporarily accompanied the dearth of Dearborn kittens. She and I never spoke of it and we continued to do battle with the amazing reproductive qualities of her feral cats.

Another woman with whom I became acquainted over a bumper crop of kittens did not end so amusingly. This lady, an apartment dweller, contacted me with the familiar dilemma of having a cat of which her landlord did not approve. I could hear the tears in her voice as she told me how Tabitha had gotten out one time and then turned up pregnant a month later. What was she going to do, the woman wondered. Now she was going to have not one illegal cat but a whole family of them.

I told her I would take Tabitha until she'd delivered and raised her kittens and then I would return her cat to her – spayed. She vowed to find another place to live in the meantime, one that would allow her to have a pet. I took the cat and housed her for the three months necessary to restore her to her previous nonpregnant condition.

I talked to the woman from time to time during the process and she claimed she was having no luck in securing a new apartment in a more pet-friendly building. I should have realized there was something not kosher about this person when she continued to tell me she hadn't yet moved and it was nearing the time to return Tabitha.

"What do you want me to do?" I inquired. "I can find her another home if you can't take her back."

"No, I love Tabitha," she wailed. "I couldn't bear to give her away. Can you give me just another month before you give her away?"

I agreed. She seemed relieved but, a month later, had still not relocated. I wound up finding a nice home for Tabitha with an older lady who'd just lost her 19-year-old tabby to cancer. I thought it was a good outcome for all and called the original owner to tell her of the happy ending.

"You what?!" She was beside herself. "You gave my cat away? How could you do that? You knew I was going to move into a new apartment."

"But I thought we agreed," I started. I clearly remembered coming to this conclusion with her blessing.

"I didn't agree to any such thing," she insisted, noticeably angry. "How dare you take my cat from me! You can't just decide to do that without asking me. Where is she? I want her back."

Feeling like a horrible person, I commenced to explain to her that the new owner was already attached to Tabitha and that, after all, she still had not moved as she'd planned and had promised to do. Didn't she think it was for the best that her cat remained where she was?

But there was no consoling her and she wound up hanging up on me, determined to make me sorry I had dared to deprive her of her cat.

Anonymous messages started to appear on social media about what a bad rescue operation Other Mothers was. "This woman stole my cat," one of the posts accused. "She is not a hero. She is a cat thief."

I tried to reach out to her at the most recent phone number I had but it seemed she had finally moved away and changed her number in the process. The negative posts continued for a period of months and finally dwindled off. I couldn't figure out how the misunderstanding could have occurred. It continued to bother me until I finally came to the only partially satisfying conclusion that, no matter what you do, some people are going to be upset with you in this line of work. Human nature was a funny thing. I really believe this woman was convinced that I had done her wrong. I had to grow a thicker skin.

THE INCONVENIENCE OF DYING

Since I had always been very literal, I could neither assimilate nor adapt. I wasn't good at schmoozing or mingling. This I blamed on my strange army childhood during which I never learned any social skills. I chose to believe the reason I was successful in working with animals was that people could tell I was authentic. They knew there was no guile in me, that this was really who I was. They knew, for the most part, that I wouldn't take advantage of them or steer them wrong. Even though I had made a mess of most of my life, I'd found something – just the right something – that I was good at. And, for this, I was grateful.

Klaus had told me many times that I was crazy. And I know he has always meant it in a good way. I was a depressive. That much has been well-documented. And I thought that I probably suffered from either borderline or avoidant personality disorder, too, as well as PTSD from my aforementioned dysfunctional childhood. Admittedly, the majority of these maladies were self-diagnosed. Mainly, I just do things differently than other people and that was usually okay. Or at least *I* was okay with it. Now that I was single and officially retired, I was reconciled to the fact that I probably wasn't meant to be part of a couple or of a corporation. I could function to the extent that I got done what needed to be done with a minimum of trouble either to myself or to those with whom I came in contact. My world view was wabi sabi, the Buddhist acceptance of transience and imperfection. That, and the love of my animals and my family, made this a good life in spite of my diagnoses. Sometimes, people thought I didn't care. That wasn't it. I just had to keep my emotions tuned to low as an act of self-preservation.

I got a call one Thursday night as I was finishing up the animal chores. My dad was in the hospital. He had fallen down at home and had suffered internal bleeding due to the large daily dose of warfarin he was on to combat a cardiac arrhythmia. Once in the hospital they gave him three blood transfusions and waited to see if it would get better on its own. It didn't.

It was no mystery that I cringed every time the phone rang. Phone calls brought death and despair. I tended to conduct most of my business by text and email rather than busy myself on the phone. The way it demanded my attention unnerved me.

By the time I got there, he was feeling ornery and combative. I didn't stay long. It was too hard to watch him struggling and only half-understanding what was being done to him. They decided to perform an endoscopy even though, due to his age, the doctors didn't think it was a good idea to do too much in the way of intrusive procedures. I went back home to wait for the results of the test.

My mom was clearly having an alternate dialogue with reality. She completely blew over the part the doctor said about my dad possibly not getting any better or even not surviving the endoscopy. They seemed to think he was in poor condition in general quite aside from his fall. He was dehydrated, had pneumonia, the aforementioned bleeding, and he was having trouble swallowing. My mom seemed to think he would feel better in a couple of days and be on his way home. Somehow, I didn't think it was going to work out that way this time.

Dr. Wong called back just two hours later. They'd already done the procedure and found nothing. She said that was good news. However, he was still anemic and they didn't know why, so I wasn't sure what had been gained. I informed my mom. It was hard to tell whether she was able to understand any of it. She seemed to get it and then she would go off on a tangent about one thing or another that had nothing to do with the issue at hand. Klaus thought she had a need to underplay the seriousness of his situation in order to deal with it emotionally. Maybe so. But now, this time, she had to be able to take it all in in no uncertain terms. Otherwise, she wouldn't be prepared to take care of him if and when they sent him home.

In the meantime, the hospital decided to release my dad to a short-term rehabilitation facility so he could continue to get stronger and improve his cognition, which had suffered during his overall trauma. I didn't know whether they had gotten him better in the hospital or had just given up on him. Whatever the case, the first night at the rehab clinic, he wandered outside and had to be brought back in and, no doubt, chastised for breaking the rules. Can you imagine, a grown man not allowed to go outside? How irate would *you* be? I felt bad for him. But he was likely to fall again if he walked around by himself.

One morning after some self-help by Google, I called Klaus to tell him what I'd learned, that I thought our dad was dying.

"Why do you think that?" he asked. "Other than the fact that he's almost a hundred years old?"

Dear Klaus. Always a practitioner of the obvious.

"I looked up the signs of impending death on the computer," I said. "And dad has most of them."

I took a breath and forged ahead.

"Remember how mom said he hadn't eaten for a couple of days before he fell? Loss of appetite is the first sign. Then there's excessive fatigue and sleeping. He has that too."

"Anything else?"

"Yes, there's an increase in physical weakness. And periods of mental disorientation. Both of which he's been experiencing in spades. And labored breathing. Changes in urination. Swelling of the feet and legs. Check, check and check. The only ones he doesn't have, that I know of, are coolness in the extremities and mottled veining."

"He has been getting really cold lately," Klaus added. "Yesterday when I was visiting him, he had four blankets on him and just couldn't get warm."

"I don't know."

"I don't know either."

"What do we do?"

I don't know.

"I don't know either."

"Well," I said, "They've got him wearing diapers, for christsakes. I just don't think he's getting any better."

"I don't see what we can do," Klaus said. "He'll either get better or he won't."

Helpless, we left it at that until the facility called the next morning to say he'd developed a rash in his groin area and they were treating it with an antibiotic cream. This was the kind of thing you had no business knowing about your dad. But I had to be on the receiving end of all such calls since they'd decided my mom was so out of it that she couldn't be the contact person.

Then at some point, apropos of absolutely nothing, my mother became convinced they were not giving my dad his prescribed medications. She wanted to move him to another facility. I tried to talk her into discussing her concerns with the rehab staff first. She said she would and then asked me when he would get to come home. I told her I didn't know and that she should ask his doctor when he went to his upcoming appointment. Unfortunately, the rehab clinic was transporting him to his appointment and neither Klaus nor I would be able to attend. As his immediate next of kin, my mom would have to receive and convey any necessary information.

He was clearly getting worse instead of better. I didn't know what to do. This called for a quickie trip to Vegas. A short gambling junket would restore my soul. Klaus would stay home and provide whatever support our mom and dad needed. My daughter Dinah would hold down the fort and take care of the animals. It would just be me and those video keno machines. God help me.

My mom was literally making my dad crazy. It frustrated me the way she tried to control every little detail: where he put his slippers, when he got dressed, whether he could have coffee, on and on it went for no earthly reason – except that she had a need to maintain control over the situation. Dad became increasingly agitated and stressed by all the pointless fussing. I kept trying to tell her that the more he did on his own, the better he would be. If he wanted to put on his pants, help him do it. If he wanted Neosporin on his knees, help him put it on. I was at the point where I felt I just couldn't take it anymore. I decided that when I returned from my trip I would try to visit him at times when my mother wasn't present. I wasn't even the object of all the fussing and it was driving *me* crazy.

Leaving Dinah in charge of the animals was both a blessing and a curse. She loved them and took excellent care of every detail. But, with her anxiety disorder, it stressed her to the point of distraction. She constantly catered to them, believing they needed something from her at every moment. It exhausted her physically and left her emotionally off kilter for days. I tried to let her know the critters could do with a minimum of attention while I was away but she wasn't getting the point. I knew I would return home to find multiple dog beds in every room, lots of enticing options in the cat food pantry and new toys for all of them. And, by gosh, those litter boxes would be pristine. But Dinah would be a nervous wreck.

It seemed that I blinked and was back at home. I returned on the red-eye the night before and already had calls waiting from my mom. The rehab facility had decided my dad couldn't be further helped by continued therapy, so Medicare was cutting him off. Unless he moved to a facility that had a contract with the Veterans Administration, he would have to pay. My parents were not comfortable shelling out $600 a day for *any* reason. I filed an appeal, but it didn't look too good. My mom was ready to yank my dad out of there and bring him home immediately.

She had to go to Fred Meyer to pick up "a few things" that would overfill my trunk. I wrangled her walker into the back seat and got her all settled and belted in.

"Do you think the VA would send someone over to the house to take care of your dad?" She was feeling out her options.

"You can't bring dad home. He's not ready." She didn't respond to anything less than blunt clarity and, besides, as I already mentioned, finesse was not my strong suit. "Anyway, the VA doesn't provide round-the-clock nursing care. We've already talked about that."

"Right. Do you think we could stop at Burger King? I want to get some French fries."

It was the most supreme of ironies. As a fat kid, I grew up forbidden to have French fries either because I was a fat kid or because my parents were just that cheap. I was never sure which it was. Now I'd wound up giving them to my mother, in her dotage, to feed this huge French fry monkey she had on her back. When I was ten, I would have killed for a French fry. Now I didn't even want to look at them.

"Yes, you can have fries. But let's go to the store first," I try bargaining with her.

"But I'm hungry. Can't we go now?" I guess delayed gratification wasn't her strong suit either. "I have a coupon."

"Okay. We'll go now." I hung a big U turn and started down the opposite way toward Burger King. It was a beautiful day. I could smell eucalyptus in the air. Usually you could only smell the acrid sawmill smell from the other side of town. "Burger King, here we come."

"You don't mind, do you?"

"No, I don't mind."

"Good. Can you come back down tomorrow?"

"What for? Is there something we can't get done this afternoon?" It was an hour and a half drive between where I lived and where she lived and I didn't relish making the trip two days in a row unnecessarily.

"Well, I want to drive by this other nursing home so I'll know where it is. In case they have to move your dad."

"Let's just wait and see what happens first. Once there's a decision on the appeal, we'll go from there."

"Don't forget my fries. Burger King is coming up on the left."

"I got this, mom. See? I'm turning in now."

"*At home* people took care of their family members themselves. There was no such thing as a nursing home." She dug in her purse, presumably for the coupon.

I didn't like where she was going with this. By 'at home,' she meant back in Germany. She used this term fairly randomly when she didn't like the way I was doing things. Who knew what they did with their old people in 1930's Germany? They didn't exactly have the best human rights track record. I thought it better to just let this one go.

Her fries procured, we went on to buy the groceries, pick up prescription refills at the drive-thru pharmacy, stop at the bakery for 'those good, soft oatmeal cookies' ("You know I can't eat store cookies with my teeth.") and I even found time to drive by the new nursing home. It was a nondescript one-story building in a residential neighborhood next to an elementary school. The benefit of driving by was negligible but my mom seemed satisfied. For the moment.

I fully expected my appeal to be denied. Then the shit would really hit the fan. Dad was going to flip out about moving to another nursing home. He would demand that we just take him home. But he couldn't even get up by himself to use the bathroom and my mom certainly couldn't lift him. It might be better to just not be present when it was time to move him. Better to let the staff tell him and let them deal with the consequences. After all, he couldn't just get up and storm out under his own steam.

I dropped off my mom, waited until she was settled in her chair with a bowl of Doritos and a glass of apple juice. Then I headed out to the casino for a little keno therapy. A couple hundred dollars down, I considered it a fair deal for taking my mind off the growing debacle with the parents. I headed back up to Portland. It had started to rain and traffic was thick with people all heading home after their workday. I hoped there would be no phone messages waiting for me.

When I arrived home, it was almost 9 o'clock and I was beyond tired. I was doing a low carb diet, trying to get down to under 200 pounds. So, looking forward to an evening of TV news and meat, I was rummaging through the refrigerator when Dinah came in.

"Hi sweetie. How was your day?" I asked. "What did you do today?"

"Don't ask me. I can't stand your questioning everything I do. It was fine, okay?"

"Okay."

"I'm going to Frank's tonight. I just need to get something to eat first and to pack a bag. How was Grandpa today?"

"Same as before. And your grandma is all worked up. She thinks they're going to boot him out into the street."

"They're not, are they?" She stopped in her march down the hallway.

"No, of course not. We've got everything under control."

She took in this answer and mulled it over for a moment. "You're a good daughter," she said.

"Thank you."

I really meant it. I was trying so hard.

When I entered my room, the dogs wagged their tails and hopped up and down. They were always there when I needed them. Even the cats seemed mildly pleased to see me, although it was really kind of hard to tell. But sometimes, because of them, the day ended just right. And this was one of those days.

My dad never got better. He died a week later. He had a military service at the veterans' cemetery. They played Taps and laid him to rest like a hero. And in a way, he was. He was a man who always did what he was supposed to do. As someone who rarely did, I thought there was an element of heroism in that.

LYING DOWN WITH DOGS

The phone rang twice and I recognized the number so I answered it on the third ring. "Hello?"

"Hi, Linda." It's Debbie at Clackamas County. "How's it going?"

"It's going well. How are you?"

"You know. SSDD." She snorted a little bit when she laughed. "Well, you probably know why I'm calling."

"My guess would be it's about that Doberman you guys confiscated. Am I right?"

Debbie had contacted me a couple of weeks prior about a pregnant Doberman Pinscher that belonged to a man who was put in jail pending trial for beating up his girlfriend.

"You're right," Debbie said. "Well, it seems the scumbag took a plea deal and he'll be going away for a couple of years. Now we officially own this dog. Can you take her?"

Something told me I should look a gift horse in the mouth in this case. "Does she happen to have any behavioral problems?" I asked.

"Just a couple." Debbie took a deep breath. "I'd be willing to bet this guy was abusing his dog as well as his girlfriend. She's afraid of sudden movements, thunder and men wearing hats. To name just a few things that we've discovered so far. But, other than that, she's a sweetheart. Honest."

"I'll bet." I knew I wasn't going to turn her down. "When can I come out and meet this charming lady?"

We made plans to get together the following morning at the county shelter.

In the meantime, I would have to go out to the shed and drag in the kiddy wading pool that I'd been using as a whelping pen for my bigger dogs. I would also have to stock up on puppy chow to feed the pregnant girl and grab a couple of stacks of the free newspaper from the stand in front of Buster's. I considered for a bit and thought I had everything else I might need for the new dog.

Since she was skittish, I was going to house her in my bedroom with me. Scarlet and Sophie would have to move to the living room for a while. They knew the drill. They didn't like it, but they always got used to their temporary relocation when I had a new mom in my room.

"Dinah, guess what. I'm getting a new dog."

"I figured," she replied, with just a tad of sarcasm in her voice. "From the way you were tromping up and down the hallway."

"You don't mind, do you?" I always had to ask. I tried to be thoughtful since she was living here too and a new dog always brought a certain level of inconvenience to the household.

"No, it's okay. Did I hear you say it was a Doberman? I hope she's friendly."

"Me too." I said, thinking that a lot of this had to be figured out on the fly. "Me too."

The next morning, I stopped at Starbucks for my coffee and got a blueberry scone to eat on the hour-long drive. I had a blanket in the backseat as I knew this mom wouldn't fit into a small-to-medium kennel. I sure hoped she liked riding in the car.

One of these days I was going to have to stop buying Honda Civics and get myself something larger in order to better accommodate my lifestyle. There were always animals to haul, large supplies of dog food and cat litter, and the occasional piece of junk shop furniture to bring home. None of the above fit easily into the Civic but I was a confirmed Honda person. I spent the drive looking at people driving Honda-made SUVs on the freeway. I don't know. I just didn't care for the way they looked. Too station wagony, I thought.

I got to the shelter and pulled into a spot close to the door. I looped the leash around my shoulders, grabbed my big purse, and went in looking for Debbie. She was in the office waiting for me so we took care of the transfer paperwork up front and went back to the runs to fetch our dog.

"Her name is Delilah. She's a real sweetheart." Debbie said.

"Yes, I believe you mentioned that." I was a bit dubious but followed her back. "Do you know if she likes car rides? I couldn't fit a large enough carrier into my car."

"I really don't know. We've had her for a good long while waiting for the owner's case to resolve but that's one thing we haven't... Oh, here she is." Delilah was as lovely as her name. She was calm and attentive when we walked up. I was sure she was going to be a barker but she didn't utter a sound, just looked at us curiously.

"Hi Delilah. Hey buddy. Want a treat?" I said bending over to her level. I always carried a pocketful of dog treats the better to make friends with my new dogs. She was sleek and black with a brown face and brown paws. She gently took the treat through the kennel bars. "What a good girl."

"She looks so thin. Are you guys sure she's pregnant?" "Yes," Debbie said. "The vet did an X-ray. It was still too early to tell how many there are but she's definitely pregnant. She does look like she's missed a few meals but I'm sure you'll take care of that, right?"

"You bet. That's what I do." I adjusted my purse and slipped the lead on her when Debbie opened the kennel gate. "She seems like such a good dog."

"She really is," Debbie said. Very well-behaved. And smart too. Watch this." She turned to Delilah. "Sit girl. Good dog."

Just then one of the kennel maintenance guys came into the unit dragging a big hose. Delilah cowered down beside the gate, looking like she wanted to go back in.

"See?" Debbie started. "She's a bit of a scaredy-cat. But no snapping or growling, thank goodness. She's not at all aggressive. She passed her behavioral screen with flying colors. You know we wouldn't transfer a dangerous dog to you guys."

"Oh, I know that," I said. I knew that all their incoming dogs had to take an intensive behavioral test before they were eligible for transfer or adoption. "We'll get her used to noises and strangers in no time."

Delilah walked out to my car with perfect manners, no pulling or lunging at the leash. She was a little bit hesitant to hop into the car, but I finally convinced her to get in. Once inside, she rode quietly all the way home as if she was used to going for rides. Somebody had spent a lot of time with this dog. She was, in spite of her fears, well-socialized. Given the environment she'd come from, I was just glad she wasn't a traumatized mess. Her fears, we could work on.

Once I got her set up in my room with a fresh dish of kibble and some cold water, I sat down on my bed and started talking to her. By the end of the day, she seemed relaxed and comfortable in her new surroundings. It had to be better than a cage with a bunch of barking dogs all around her. After she'd eaten a bowlful of kibble, I took her outside where she promptly took care of her business. Whew!, I thought. I was always glad to learn they were house-trained. Especially the big ones. She stretched and curled up her long coltish legs and went to sleep in her wading pool bed.

I woke the next morning feeling a solid weight against my side. At some point, Delilah had decided it would be a good idea to climb into bed with me. I didn't know if something had scared her during the night. Perhaps the raccoon family that lived on my roof was making a racket again. Or she'd heard a siren in the distance. Nothing much disturbed me when I slept so I had to just give her the benefit of the doubt. She wasn't a snorer or a drooler, so I let her stay.

The next night she did the same thing again, crawled into my bed and got under the covers after the lights went out. She was pleasant-enough company, but this time it felt like she'd short-sheeted my bed. I readjusted everything and then went back to sleep with Delilah snoozing peacefully beside me.

It became her habit to join me every night. I got used to her warmth and she seemed to be set in her habits. I made a mental note that I would definitely have to eventually find her a home with someone who didn't mind sleeping with dogs. I knew I wasn't the only one.

Several weeks into her stay with me, I woke one night to find Delilah back in her wading pool. I turned on the light on the bedside table to find out what was wrong, and I saw that she had delivered seven perfect black puppies while I was sleeping. She was lying in her pool licking each one in turn, every bit the proud new mother.

She never got back into bed with me until her puppies were weaned and all gone to their new homes. Then she started again to creep into my bed after I fell asleep. Her fears had subsided with time, and she turned out to be the most well-mannered dog ever. There was no excessive barking or separation anxiety when I had to leave her alone at home. She became the perfect companion animal and wound up going home with a nice couple that didn't mind her curious nightly routine in the slightest.

I often wondered about the origin of her initial fears, more, how she was, underneath them, a remarkable dog. She was a bit of an enigma. I theorized that while perhaps the man had been cruel, perhaps the woman had treated Delilah with kindness. That might explain some of her behavioral quirks but of course I never found out how an abusive man had come to have such a patient and mellow dog. It was just another one of those puzzles that surprised and ultimately delighted me about my animal charges. They tend to be unbelievably resilient and forgiving. I thought, not for the first time, that we could all learn a lot from them.

A DARKNESS INSIDE

In December of 2019, I wrote in an article about compassion fatigue for Animal Wellness magazine:

"Studies have indicated that the brains of people who experienced a lot of early trauma in their lives become hardwired to respond easily and deeply. This includes people who may turn to animals for unconditional love after some acute trauma, as well as those who were termed 'sensitive children' because they lack a fundamental emotional resiliency. These are the kids who are easy to cry, suffer from excessive shyness, or are melancholy in nature, dwelling on sad thoughts and memories."

Reading that passage now, I don't recall whether I actually read that someplace or simply pulled it from some deep recess in my knowledge banks. Whichever the case, I was simply describing myself. Early trauma. Turning to animals for unconditional love. Lack of emotional resiliency. It was all there. I don't know what it had to do with compassion fatigue especially, but truer words were never spoken.

I always knew those things about myself, knew that I was a sensitive child, knew that I was prone to sadness, but I came to realize there was something more in the tossed salad of emotional inclinations that defined me. There was a darkness beyond the glum despondency, a secret sauce of black thoughts and grim proclivities, that made me who I was.

When I was ten, I drew pictures of movie monsters devouring hapless damsels. At fifteen, I haunted cemeteries. Then, as an adult, I sought out every dark alley of my mind. What was it that made me prone to such despair? It was, at least partially, that early trauma that I mentioned in the article. No one who loved me. No one to turn to. Not different, then, than many an unlucky child. But pair that with what I believe were the inherent seeds of depression swirling around in my brain and what results is a blackness like no other.

Most non-affected people don't understand what clinical depression is and what it is not. They know about the sadness but not about the hopelessness, the fatigue, the mental fog that is a part of your brain like an extra lobe. It weighs you down, blacks out the light and seals off your ability to discriminate among life's choices. Even many depressives probably don't have a firm grasp of what all is included in their malady. I lost my career to my disease, never appreciating that my inability to do my job anymore was because of it. The depression left me tired, confused, and unable to concentrate. I wasn't just sad. I was without the necessary clarity of thought to solve a problem, follow a process, or imagine a better mousetrap. Moreover, that lack made it impossible to recognize these failures within myself or to address them in a beneficial way. I was simply cast adrift in an unfamiliar landscape, one that I was previously able to navigate successfully, and which had now become a shadowy and nonlinear terrain.

I tell you these things not to be a downer or a complainer. I don't ask for your sympathy or your indulgence. I only want you to know. I want to you to hear the cry for help that I myself cannot hear. And maybe that's asking too much.

If I had blindness or a lame leg, or cancer, we would all know it and everything would be fine. I might not be able to read a document or run a race or show up every day but I would do my job to the best of my ability and that would either be okay or it wouldn't be okay. There would be no gray area. There would be no character judgements or casting of aspersions. But it occurs to me that being depressed is a lot like being fat. Everyone can see it but they tend to blame the victim. He's not trying hard enough. She's weak of will. It's their own doing. It comes down to blame. Whose fault is it then when a person loses her ability to fully function in the world? Whose fault is it that she falters and fails and can't get up again?

I know there are no excuses allowed in life. I know that each person must take responsibility for fixing what is wrong with them. But how does one fix something that evades a label, that has no bells or whistles to signify its coming, that robs a person of the judgement it takes to seek help? I ask you these things. Perhaps you will have an answer for me.

One dreary day – for every day seemed dreary – I came upon a moment of clarity. I realized that I was not the same as everyone else. I could no longer do the work that was expected of me. I could have chosen to admit it and seek help. But I was afraid. I was afraid of my own ebbing faculties. And I chose to disguise the problem. I chose to grit my teeth and bluff my way through, parroting the views and ideas of others. Sure, I know, that was a bad choice. But unsound reasoning is what depression is all about. You do it over and over again until people begin to notice. The result is that, eventually, you wind up running away from a mob of angry villagers wielding flaming torches just like in an old Frankenstein movie. The only thing that matters is getting away. Fire bad. The creature is doomed.

When one is thrice cursed – depressed, fat and a writer – well, watch out world! There's bound to be some bad shit go down. You can, and you will, tell others about how it feels. And no one wants to hear it because it's depressing and it's frustrating and it's all your fault anyway. But you soldier on and you learn to embrace the specialness of it. You come to discover your own special lens through which you can view the world like no one else can. Where there is darkness, there is nuance. Where there is confusion, there is possibility. And since no one can explain you or define you, you can learn to define yourself.

I'm not the first person to choose to interpret my malady as a gift. And it's an imprecise approach to unraveling an eventual recovery. But sometimes how you label something makes all the difference in the world, especially when you feel robbed of the ability to accurately know yourself or trust your intuition. The gift of depression is really a wake-up call. It tells us that things are not okay the way they are. It lets us know that something is not right, that instead of feeling guilt over our unhappiness, we should seek out the reasons. Maybe, even beyond that, it tells us that perhaps happiness is not what we should seek but awareness.

We spend our years hiding our inner feelings and going through the motions of being who we think we should be. Building a successful career. Being a good parent. Making money. Having friends and having lovers. But, in hiding our true feelings of hopelessness and loss, we miss the important message inherent in those dangerous feelings. We have learned that our feelings are our enemy, our Achilles heel, and we bury them deeply, choosing to do and act as we believe we should. After all, if a depressive acted on his selfish nature, he would spend his life in bed in a dormant state of nothingness. Right? Maybe not. Maybe underneath all of our self-talk and "shoulds" there is something besides the blackness we have come to recognize as our authentic self.

Underneath all the layers of worldliness that led me to believe I needed to be a certain way, I knew that my depression was not a blank slate, not a total absence of feelings. I knew it was a mask that covered those feelings because they were too dangerous. They needed to be hammered down into a bearable half-life that would allow me to thrive again at some point in the unforeseeable future. It was like playing a game of Whack-A-Mole, striking out at every errant true emotion in order to control my unhappiness and a create a perfect flat field of unemotionality. That approach worked to some extent, allowed me to be successful in ways and to avoid blowing my brains out. But maybe there was the possibility of more there. And that possibility is the thing we call hope.

Psychotherapy and medications can help us get to that place of hope. So can meditation and prayer. But, ultimately, we have to be brave enough to accept the challenge offered. We have to be willing to feel life, to get on the roller coaster and experience every jerk, every peak and every plummet. We have to venture out of the sensory deprivation tank in which we have existed and know that we will be buffeted around some.

For me, what started out as helplessness over the loss of my work life turned out to be a groping towards what I *could* do when there was much at which I had failed. At first my steps were small and tentative. I practiced a modicum of self-care, took my meds, got up every day and communed with my animals. Selfishly, I did as I wanted and needed. And I found that there was something there. My love for animals was real. My appreciation of life's little blessings – the colors of a sunrise, the sound of rain on the roof at night, the exhilaration of skipping on the sidewalk like a kid again – were all authentic parts of me.

Once I stopped hiding and acting, I found my true calling. Corporate life wasn't for me, that was clear. I wound up envisioning and starting Other Mothers Animal Rescue, a small piece of a big picture. It was what I could do to impact the world. I took those pregnant dogs out of their cages and brought them home where they could have their babies free from fear. I loved them. It was what I was meant to do. And with all the neglect and abuse in the world, life was not without sadness, without despair. I found that the highs were worth it. I had been feeling that sadness and despair anyway locked in my little cocoon, so I might as well burst out into the big, ugly world and garner some of the upside as well as the self-imposed downside.

Am I healed? No. Am I always happy? No. But I have my moments of satisfaction and of joy. I have a sense that that elusive state is not a destination but a journey. I now exist on a continuum and not in a self-dug ditch. There will always be a darkness inside me. There are a multitude of reasons and I cannot go back and un-live them. I cannot escape my past, my choices or the chemicals that swirl through my imperfect brain. I am who I am. And, for today, that is good enough.

DECLINE

It was happening again. This time it was my mom. I knew she was dying. Suddenly she was losing all of her faculties, mental as well as physical. She had fallen a couple of times and was too weak to get up. And sometimes she literally didn't know where she was. Once, I arrived at her house to find the doors unlocked and her down on the floor. She'd slid out of her chair reaching for a dropped piece of paper. And she was complaining that nobody had come to help her up.

"Where *are* these darn people?" she said. "All these employees and no one has come along to help me. And I don't know why your dad hasn't come either."

I was able to help her back onto her chair after a few false starts.

"What people? There are no people here. You're at home." I thought it was best to be frank and direct with her.

She looked around, taking in the art on the walls, the furniture, perhaps the paint colors. "Oh, that's right. I thought I was at the nursing home with your dad."

. "And, as for dad, you know he's been gone for a while now."

"Oh, that's right." At that, she sounded disappointed. It was one small chink in her armor and a slightly endearing reaction to her loss.

Hers was such a sudden decline that I didn't have time to question whether she was still safe at home alone – she wasn't – or if she should at least have someone to come in and care for her – she should. I just knew that she was dying too and, more than anything else, I felt a guilty impatience with the whole process. I thought life would be better if we were just here one day and gone the next. This terrible period of wasting away was good for nothing and just prolonged the inevitable. Not that I wished her dead per se. I just wanted her to be her old self or not to be at all. Was that so awful?

I was glad when she came up with the idea of moving into an assisted living facility. I didn't want to have to try to make her do it, but it was the only solution to the problem of her safety. Dinah thought her grandma should move in with us and I couldn't bring myself to tell her all the reasons this wouldn't work. She had been a bad mother. I couldn't bear the idea of spending the rest of my sixties taking care of her. The resentment would have been too great a price to pay for doing the right thing. Having Dinah live with me was different. She was a good daughter and a good person in many ways. And I felt I owed her. To whatever degree I might have contributed to my daughter's anxiety disorder, I wanted to do right by her.

My mom needed a referral from her doctor in order to move into a facility. Fortunately, she had a check-up scheduled and I was determined to assist her in getting what she wanted. There was one problem. My mom was likely to lie about the extent of her infirmities, by longstanding habit, just to make everything sound normal. She wouldn't stop to consider that this would defeat her purpose. This tendency toward lying seemed to me one of the aftereffects of growing up in Nazi Germany. You had to make everything sound normal to avoid scrutiny.

I said, "Mom, you've got to be truthful. Let the doctor know how bad it's gotten, that you can't get up by yourself anymore, that you forget things sometimes, and that you don't feel safe at home anymore."

She considered these things and worried aloud that if she told him, she might be committed or somehow lose her freedom of will. I assured her this would not be the case, that the doctor had no interest in keeping her a prisoner somewhere. She was dubious.

When the time came and we were called into the doctor's office, she said something like "What would you think about my moving into The Regency?" She had a way, well into her dotage, of regaining her clarity at the critical times.

Fortunately, he said he thought this was a good idea. He did go on to ask about her specific concerns and she downplayed the severity of what was happening, as I'd feared, but he seemed to intuit that the time had come. It turned out all we had to do was find a place and they would coordinate with her doctor's office to complete all the paperwork.

I thought of her all those years ago, of her willful striding toward the neighbor's homes on those summer days back in De Ridder, eager to gossip and drink Pepsi. I thought about her lack of patience with an equally willful teenage daughter and how I felt getting smacked with a hairbrush, or a wooden spoon or a coat hanger or whatever she happened to be holding in her hand. I thought about her disengaged response to my crying. Was she trying to make me strong? Didn't she know how to react? Or did she really not care? I tended to think my crying was simply something she couldn't control, something that stood in the way of her social narrative, that of the perfect family. She must have had a hell of a bad childhood herself, not just because of the bombing and the fear of the gestapo coming in the night. She must have had a bad childhood because her parents sounded as harsh and as uncaring as she turned out to be. For that fact, I had genuine empathy. It was all water under the bridge, and I didn't hold a conscious grudge but I could never forget and I would never think it was okay to have been ignored when I needed her.

I was glad she got what she wanted. I was glad that she would be safe and cared for. Most of all, I was glad I was going to outlive her, to be free of her curse at last. Now, the only thing keeping her from assisted living was her discovery that the costs would not be covered by her insurance. In light of that, she would probably end up dying in that house alone or falling and hurting herself and wind up in a nursing home. The idea that my supposed inheritance would be consumed by a retirement home didn't faze me. It was her money and it was a hell of a lot more important to her than it was to me. But there was no budging her once the reality set in that she would have to pay to live in a safe place. With her house paid for and hers to live in for free, she wasn't going anywhere.

The fact remained, and I kept coming back to it, that even a dog would rather have negative attention than no attention at all. And I was no different. True, I was never kept locked in a cage or shackled to a radiator, but I was a prisoner, nonetheless. I was a prisoner of the love that was withheld. A kid needs that love to grow and develop normally. And, lacking it, that need doesn't ever go away.

I hoped to hell I didn't do the same thing to Dinah as was done to me. I always felt that I loved her even though I wasn't too good at demonstrating it. Did she think I didn't? Did my own mother hold a similar undisplayed love toward me?

Deep relationships were too complicated for me. I didn't know how to make sense of them or deal with them. And I guess that was the whole problem. We learn by example, don't we, and the example I was shown was cold, secretive, and short-tempered. And now the tables were turned. I was in the caretaker role and my mother was the helpless child. I'm not sure I had anything to give back to her.

When my dad was dying, my mom didn't even attempt to care for him. She didn't know where his dentures were and that he had only one lens in his eyeglasses. Whether she was beyond caring or just didn't feel it was her job anymore, she wouldn't budge. She wanted him in a nursing home and she assumed correctly that his care would be covered by his veterans' benefits. Now that it was her turn, she felt entitled to the same benefits. She'd always had a hard time drawing a line between who he was and who she was. Maybe she was trying to pay him back for all those years of physical abuse. I couldn't blame her for that. She'd shown up often enough with bruises and black eyes and I knew, even as a kid, she couldn't be that clumsy. But she must have thought it was a good trade-off because she never left, never complained. She just kept her mouth shut and continued to thrive courtesy of her own personal version of the Marshall Plan. Did she sell her soul for the good life? I don't know. I only know that it was part of her demeanor to play down the beatings.

When I was a kid, my dad would regularly drink too much and become enraged. She was the one there to suffer the consequences. He never touched my brother Klaus and me. But I always thought he had plenty of reason to be angry and without any apparent outlet. I had the feeling that the root of my affinity for my dad was that, as a man, that which came out in me as hopelessness and despair, manifested itself as rage for him.

He was just a poor country kid. He'd come of age during the Great Depression and wound up leaving home to join the army. From then on, he had everything taken care of for him. The military did everything: paid his bills, gave him housing and plenty of cheap goods from the commissary – and even provided him with a bride. As a result, he never learned anything about autonomy or competitiveness or aspiration. No wonder he was frustrated. My mom was just the opposite. She came of age in pre-war Germany where you must have learned to hustle almost before you could walk. She was always looking for an angle. No wonder she was uncaring. Both of them, each in their own way, was markedly ill-equipped to raise children. But they did it anyway and wound up with a couple of kids who didn't know much of anything until they grew up and learned it the hard way.

My mother was abusive, domineering, and detached. My dad, as it turned out, was a racist. But he was always kind to me and mindful of my personal space. What a messed-up deal. But it was the deal we got, Klaus and me, for better or for worse. It was a mystery that I still felt the need to choose sides, to determine who was most to blame.

It occurred to me that, in spite of the fact that we always seemed to have distant relatives to visit on those interminable road trip vacations, ours was a small immediate family. I have a couple of first cousins out there somewhere, siblings who were the children of my dad's younger brother. Sometimes I wonder if they grew up anything like us, ignored and unadvised. Curiously, neither of them had any kids of their own. The only reason either Klaus or I reproduced was that our partners insisted on it and we were unable to provide a cogent reason why not. Speaking for both of us, it was without a doubt one of the best things that we ever did.

After my dad died, it became apparent that my mother was functionally illiterate on top of everything else. She was unable to read a letter or write a check. As the daughter, it fell to me as part of the caregiver role to handle all of her household business, a fact that she at once insisted on and resented. I recognized that I was in the same difficult position as a lot of women my age but that knowledge did little to make it any easier. Klaus wasn't much help. Like a lot of men, he had trouble dealing with anything that he was powerless to fix. Maybe he had more in common with our dad than he knew. Either way, it was a fine mess. I held a lot of resentment at first until I realized that was only making things worse. These people were who they were. Not only did I have to deal with it but they had not prepared me for any of it. These were matters, literally, of life and death. I was working up high and without a net. I knew I had to cut myself some slack or I would short circuit, blow another gasket and wind up in the same condition as I had been in with my ill-fated career. I had to do what I could and let the rest go.

I tried to make light of the fact that my family idea of tradition meant stopping in Bordertown on the drive home from Reno. The culture to which we aspired as a family was whatever convoluted ideal my mom embraced at any time. She was from Europe. We were raised to believe that bestowed some special cultural significance on her and, secondarily, on us. What passed for values were only the reflexes by which we hoped to survive without letting on that we were troubled, to keep up appearances, to fall in line with the current ways of reacting to things. Again, Klaus was better at it than I was. And my mom was the master. After all, it was her system. She'd put all the rules in place. My dad and I, we didn't fare so well somehow.

So, with dad gone, she sat there in that dark house alone with all the shades pulled down. Just her and her money. It was no wonder she was going crazy. And maybe it was better that she spent so much time in her dream world when the reality was so dreadful. I couldn't help but think maybe it was better than she deserved. No matter. That was how it all ended up and I felt somehow set adrift. Already in my mid-sixties, I was still ill-prepared to face life. The years came and went, punctuated by events that should have been either blessings or devastations but instead were no more than blips on a timeline. I maintained the flat affect of a depressive through it all. If nothing could phase me at all, then nothing could hurt me.

My mom died just days after we'd talked her into moving to a care facility. She didn't like it and she was determined she wouldn't be staying there for long. In a convoluted way, she got her way once again. She was buried with my dad at the Veteran's cemetery under a brass nameplate that was inscribed "Together Eternally." I didn't know if that was a good thing or not but, when pressed, it was the only truism Klaus and I could come up with when ordering the nameplate.

LESSONS LEARNED

In over twenty-five years with Ensign Insurance, you would have thought I would have developed a tougher hide. But I never did and that was what led up to or helped to facilitate my ultimate breakdown. One day in my office, I started to cry and I just couldn't stop. That was it. I had to go. Sayonara. Arrivederci. Adios. Time to go. I mean, there was more to it than that, a raft of details, misplaced blame and failed accountabilities, enough to last a lifetime. But none of it really mattered. The bottom line was simply that I couldn't do it anymore.

To say my career failed was a massive understatement. It imploded like an obsolete Las Vegas casino and, even now, through years of hindsight, I couldn't quite identify the specific reasons. I knew that, as a depressive, I had trouble with focusing, couldn't concentrate and, in general, couldn't think very well. As a result, I failed to follow instructions, solve problems and identify emergent issues. And, as I mentioned earlier, my performance grew worse and worse until I simply couldn't fake it any longer. The lens of time made it all look simple. Looking back is what it all boiled down to, trying to analyze that period of time, trying to learn from it. But I guess, after all my efforts to understand it, the only lesson I learned for sure was humility.

If indeed the definition of success is meeting failure after failure without any loss of enthusiasm, then maybe there *was* no grand enlightenment to be found, only the hope of retaining enough passion to go on to the next thing. And that seems not the same, but dangerously close, to doing the same thing over and over in the same way while expecting different results. The definition of crazy. And that's what I was trying to escape so I found that possibility unacceptable. I had to keep looking for newer, better, different means of doing things. So long as I could do that, I could continue to move forward.

I had identified ways of operating that satisfied this criteria of differentness, enough so that I could always find some excitement in what was to come. At the crossroads before starting Other Mothers, there was definitely sufficient ardor so as to make the enterprise worthwhile. I have to think this reservoir of enthusiasm was mostly medically induced. It would only serve me so long as I continued to take my meds. And that was okay. That was progress. The idea that I was one pill away from an ineffectual stupor just wouldn't do.

So, medication was an answer. Or part of an answer. The simple fact of aging had something to do with finding wisdom as well. If you lived long enough, experienced enough of life, then you might come away with a kind of wisdom even if it wasn't what you'd thought passed for wisdom when you were younger. Or was it just the sweet delusion of thinking things made sense now that never made sense before? That couldn't be true. There has to be some benefit of growing older besides simply breaking down and getting ready for the grave. There must be a reason that we don't just live and then die without ever wearing out. If not wisdom, then what?

And aging is such a strange process, really. Inside myself, I was still the same as I was for that fleeting instant when I was a young woman. I can imagine falling in love and all that that entails, for instance, but who wants to fall in love with an old woman? Perhaps an old man. And that wasn't good enough for me. I wanted a counterpart who had on the outside all the trappings that I had on the inside. Nothing less would do. I remained alone. Waiting for some perfect love that defied age and time and common sense. And alone was okay, usually, if you liked yourself and your own company. And I generally did. As long as you could hang onto a passion for life, whether or not you have someone to share it with, you're ahead of the game. I believed this to be true.

Lessons? Hell, it wasn't always fun to learn them, not always even an advantage. There was something to be said for being young and stupid after all. Oblivion was infinitely better than seeing your body sag and your ears grow large, better than being called ma'am and needing help standing up when you've thoughtlessly sat down on the floor. Oblivion was better than that and it's what we're all headed toward anyway so we might as well embrace it, right? But I wasn't ready yet and so I embarked on my latest ill-conceived adventure. I decided to write a mystery novel. Against all odds, I sat down at my computer and banged out a rough draft in a little under a month. Was it any good? Who knew? I worked out all the perceived kinks in the plot and doctored my grammar and usage to the point where I deemed the project finished. Then came the real work. I had to find out how to get the thing published.

While that project sat abandoned in my computer memory, I embarked on a different path toward publication. I had had some success in the past, a travel story in The Oregonian, winning first place in a short fiction contest, and a couple of how-to's in the animal magazines, and I liked the way they made me feel. Recognized. Accepted. Acknowledged. I decided to write a series of essays and have them published in the literary journals or, really, whichever publications would take them. Some way through this process, I felt that I had a book on my hands, a memoir of a person failing and getting up and failing again. The meaning of life as it were. But no one wants to read about a person's failures, do they? It was too depressing. I struggled along with this germ of an idea until I realized that, taken all together, I had succeeded at least as many times as I had failed.

My successes were more ephemeral, far less material, than my failures. But they were successes nonetheless. I had traveled. I had learned about life. I had endured. And these were all good things. But there was still something left unrealized. Always. A need to do something more with the life I had been given. And I think that's the secret of a life well-lived. You have to continue to aspire. A life is never a finished product. Not while one continues to have the consciousness of introspection. There was always more. More to be experienced and more to be learned.

What's next? I will travel to Africa and be afraid that I have ventured too close to the Somalian border or the Ebola regions of the Congo. I will overspend. I will despair. I may fall in love. I will read books and see films that inspire me. I will wonder about death. I will hang onto my health and my outlook for as long as is humanly possible. I will live.

I had buried both of my parents and the year of loss was finally at an end when COVID left me alone with the phantoms of their passing. There was no closure. There was only the lingering sting of a lifetime of yearning and hurt. All that I had accomplished and all that I was working toward with the animal rescue stopped abruptly when the virus hit. It was just me, alone, and my memories.

Every day was a mirror of the one that had gone before. I read and puttered around the house, missing my life of dogs, and wondering when things might get back to normal. The casinos were closed so my one source of distraction had been cut off. After two months of mourning and nothingness, I couldn't take it anymore. I had reorganized my books and planted a shelf full of plants. I had done a couple of paintings. I had sifted through my lifetime of photographs looking for what went wrong.

There were so few things that I could control these days that it was strangely satisfying to have complete mastery over something – even if it was just a closet or a refrigerator. And, though there was talk of some sort of phased reopening, it didn't seem that anything was going to change any time soon. At least it didn't seem advisable to move in that direction. After just a few months of self-imposed isolation, I believed in some deep place that this was the new normal.

Where once I had longed for a life of solitude and books, now it was happening for real and I was hungry to meet a smile with one of my own, to shake a hand, or to make meaningless small talk. And I yearned for the open road. I was well past overdue for a road trip and nothing was currently in the planning stages. I didn't know if I would ever again board a plane with that pleasant anticipation of going someplace new. It seemed unlikely.

Now there were only fearful trips to the grocery store, masked and slathered with disinfectant, with eyes downcast and ever mindful of that crucial six feet of distance between the next nearest human and me. There were drive-through errands to conduct banking and pick up food. There was the strained shouting of instructions to my lawn guy self-distancing at the edge of the carport. If I could, I would have given him a big hug and whispered to him to trim the azaleas. Wouldn't he be surprised at this new intimacy between us? But maybe he wouldn't. Maybe he would understand. Maybe he would take my hand and guide me among the rose bushes to share his handiwork. God, it was hard to realize that it wasn't just me who was isolated. It was everyone. And no one among us knew what to make of it.

But the truth was, or seemed to be, that the days of isolation were narrowing to a close. There was more talk of the reopening of cities. Did people really believe life would go on as during the pre-COVID days? Wasn't it all too obvious that social distancing and the flattening of the curve were one and the same? Didn't they realize that once people were free to interact again, the virus would return with a vengeance? It was easy to ignore these truths. We all wanted normalcy. But it would surely come at the cost of many lives.

Selfishly, I'd already determined that I would make good use of that sweet spot between summer 2020 and the dreaded viral winter. I would make hay while the sun shone and not look back. I thought that by year-end we would all be sequestered in our homes again, shell-shocked and wondering what had happened. For now, I followed the reopening of stores, of services, and of casinos. I was going to make use of them while they lasted.

I didn't want to catch the virus. At my age, I was old enough to be in the high-risk group. I'd had a tube stuck down my throat before following my weight loss surgery and I didn't plan on having that happen again. It was miserable, choking, drooling, and feeling like death. I couldn't handle it again. If I were lucky, I would get a mild case. That would be okay. Then, presumably, I would have antibodies and would possibly be immune to catching it again. Presumably.

The problem was I couldn't choose my fate. I couldn't be afraid of death anymore. When it was my turn, I would have to face it with more dignity that my mother had, more awareness than my father had, and more wisdom than my other dead had. Death. I didn't know when it would come for me and I was determined not to lose sleep waiting up for it. When it came, it came. I had a life to live now.

It just might be that my weight and my addictions and my mental deficiencies didn't really matter a whole lot in the grand scheme of things. What mattered happened in the church of now. Living was my religion, doing was my worship. I was determined to be more appreciative of those things that I could do, day in and day out, to make my life a success. And that being a relative term, I chose to define success by the actions I took, the sunsets I noticed, and the tasks I completed.

There was still so little to believe in in terms of our status in the pandemic. Was it over? Would it recur? Would we all succumb? Would we all survive? And what of the touted vaccine? There were many questions left unanswered or, rather, they were answered with lies and assumptions.

Then there was that matter of the tumor in my head. It was not malignant but was precariously placed. It would require brain surgery or radiation treatment. My choice. I talked the neurologist into an extra 6 months of lead time by opting for an additional MRI to document the tumor's growth. I would need that time, I told myself, to have a will drawn up and to prepare my daughter for the possibility that I might not survive the surgery. Terrific. Once again, the vicissitudes of life had conspired against me.

I was determined to get past this too and go on with my idyllic existence of saving animals and traveling the world. I realized how much I would miss my life and I wanted to live. But I was sixty-five, would be sixty-six at the time of the surgery. Though my parents had both lived until their late nineties and I always planned on emulating their longevity, maybe that wasn't to be in my case. Maybe this was all there was. This new development sure brought perspective to my depression and to my general cavalier outlook. I didn't want to die. Not this way. Not now.

I missed hearing the pitter-patter of tiny feet around the house. For two years in a row, in spite of my outreach efforts, no mama dogs had been sent my way. I attributed this to the fact that more shelters and state agencies were relying on foster families to house their special-needs dogs, which is a category that seemed to fit for the ones that were received in a pregnant condition. Instead of kenneling them, they were being sent home with volunteers who cared for the mom and raised the puppies. That way, the shelters were able to take advantage of the income inherent in adopting out those cute puppies. That was bad for me. Or, in a way, I could consider my efforts a success. I had been of service for about fifteen years and now I had pretty much made myself obsolete.

After two years of no babies, I think I could pretty well conclude that my Other Mothers days were over. Oh, there would still be the occasional case that came my way, I believed, but there would never be the volume of puppies I'd experienced in the past. I could only move on to something new. I wasn't sure yet about the next chapter in my life. It would involve animals. It would involve travel. I still had to make it over to Mother Africa. That was really the one big item on my "bucket list." Otherwise, I've already had a full life. Okay, so there was no graceful aging in the arms of my perfect man, no grandbabies, none of the conventional attachments to the world that will last after I am gone. But I could say that I had changed people for the better. And that is the energy that will outlive me. I have made people happy by introducing dog love into their lives. There's no finer accomplishment in my opinion.

Maybe I could switch up my emphasis and forge ahead with old dogs, blind dogs or three-legged dogs. Who knows? Maybe I could move to another city and find there the need that once existed in Portland.

For the time being, with my mom and dad both gone and the past just a dingy stain on what remained of my life, I was freer than I had been in years. And I planned to take advantage of that freedom. Only it wasn't easy to be in that state of flux. I'd always before had things that I had to do: behave myself, raise my child, manage my career, see to the elders, clean up after my puppies. It had been a long time since I had found myself at loose ends and I wasn't sure it was a happy thing. I longed to jump into something, almost anything, that would give me a reason to get up in the morning. After all that had happened to me as a kid, and all that I had missed in my earlier life, I wasn't good at just being. I had to apply myself.

Not one to rest on my laurels, I threw myself into my writing, which had always been a part of my life since childhood. I had written short stories, magazine articles, travel pieces, a novel and some essays – all with a modicum of success if success was measured in publication – but now I was starting to work on my first memoir. This new project was to be a bit of background about my early life and how I came to be the person I am today and then the story of Other Mothers Animal Rescue. I wanted people to know that they too could do what I had done, to give them the idea of going after their dreams in a way that was impactful and not beyond the capabilities of any person of normal intelligence and resourcefulness.

So that is what I did.

FURTHER COMPLICATIONS

Six months down the road from my first MRI I learned that the tumor was growing. I was going to have to choose between brain surgery and radiation treatments. I would never get to Africa at this rate. I had survived eye surgery without complication but was told by the doctors that the fix for my acoustic neuroma was a "big surgery." I made the assumption that meant it was one that I might or might not survive. I got all the information I could gather from both the surgeon and the oncologist and ultimately chose to undergo radiation.

I am not a religious person. I believe in the magic of the natural world. And, yes, at times I curse it. It can be stubborn and arbitrary with its gifts. But I think it is all we have. That and pure, blind luck – in which I am also a believer.

By this time I had learned that life charts its own path for each of us, that if we ever want to do something, the time is now because we never know what's going to happen. Between my illness and the emergence of the COVID-19 virus, I felt like I was living my life in shackles (and a mask). Since I had always traveled before when I needed respite, I chose to book myself a cabin in the woods for a couple of relatively safe weeks of rest and contemplation.

Despite my love of nature, I'm not exactly a cabin-in-the-woods type of girl. I generally prefer a trip to an exciting place that features a good deal of activity for my tourist dollar – say Las Vegas, New Orleans or New York City. However, in light of the limitations the virus had placed on us, and the fact that I had a major writing project to work on, I decided to do something I rarely do. I decided to spend two weeks alone with myself in the woods. Would I get a lot of writing done? Would I be bored to tears? Would I turn feral? Who knew? I knew only that I was willing to give it a try because it was something novel and new.

The weeks ahead of the trip were like most others in terms of making lists, notifying friends and family, and leaving my daughter with exhaustive instructions on watering the houseplants. I saved packing for the final day so I wouldn't accumulate a bunch of unnecessary stuff in my suitcase. It was my plan to pack light. Just the bare essentials. I intended to stop at the last outpost of civilization – that would be Eugene - to stock up on groceries and head from there into the forest. I believed that my trusty Euro-bag would serve me well on this trip as it had on countless others. I got the bag online from the travel writer Rick Steves' brand of travel luggage and it was a marvel of canvas engineering with a pocket or nook for every little thing I could conceivably hope to carry with me. So, between the Euro-bag and a cardboard box full of groceries, I hoped I would be amply provisioned for a fortnight in the wilderness.

Arriving at last at the cabin, though it was remote, I found myself a bit taken aback by the amenities. It had a fully equipped kitchen, central air, and a propane-burning fireplace. There was, alas, no TV and I was accustomed to relaxing, sleeping, and writing with the drone of that dreadful machine in the background. This was going to be different. But perhaps that was just what I needed. I settled in, ready for day after productive day of writing.

The first morning, I awoke from a disturbing dream in which I had taken on a foster child that was in turn, as is the way of dreams, a human baby and a beagle pup. I found myself exhaustively shopping for the child and rushing around from one government office to the next to fill out paperwork. This was the first notion I'd had that my years of caring for puppies had something to do with the rearing of human children. Did I wish I'd had more kids? Did I want a second shot at raising my daughter? Or was the dream just a reminder of how much I cared for my fur babies? All I knew was that, in the dream, I was dreadfully inept at my task, constantly dropping the child or accidentally leaving him someplace and then having to go back and find him. I was ill-equipped to care for my young, be they human or canine, this was for sure. It wasn't exactly a self-confirming dream. And it was one of those dreams that stayed with me throughout the day, coming back to haunt me at several times in both the morning and into the late afternoon.

By evening the dream was just an uncomfortable memory and I was able to buckle down to my writing and crank out a few pages. They were crap. I kept them anyway so as not to have to call the day a total loss.

By the second morning, I was ready to drive the hundred-plus miles to the nearest casino. But I didn't give in to the temptation. I took my computer out onto the screened-in porch and worked for several hours. But it was like the scene from The Shining where Jack Nicholson writes hundreds of pages of "All work and no play makes Jack a dull boy." I didn't know. Perhaps I needed the diversions of home in order to string together a garland of meaningful words. The cats hacking up hairballs. The dogs barking at sounds in the street. Dinah bewailing her lot in life. But I wasn't ready to give up yet. I had a full two weeks to fill and nothing at hand to occupy my days except the writing project.

On the third day, I hit my stride. I went back to the dream and found myself wondering if all the creative efforts I'd spent a lifetime pursuing – my writing, gardening, cooking, jigsaw puzzles, the rearing of animals – were just me trying over and over again to successfully succor a child. Whether a savory casserole or a perfect red rose, were they all just aspects of Dinah that I had been reworking over the years? If only I had it all to do over again. There were surely things I would do differently, I thought, but the bottom line was surprisingly comforting. I had done the best job of it that I possibly could at the time and the result was no less than spectacular. Sure, Dinah had an anxiety problem to which I might or might not have contributed, but she was a kind, generous, intelligent woman that I wouldn't have traded for all the Rhodes scholars and beauty queens in the world. Case closed.

For the next several days, I opened the back doors and felt the crisp, clean air against my skin as I sat typing. The sound of the river rapids was more conducive to my efforts than the TV ever had been and I found myself electrified by the nearness of nature in all its glory. But I wasn't getting precisely to the point which was what I had learned from a lifetime of missteps. Maybe I had learned nothing. Or maybe I had learned a lot but just couldn't put it into words. What good was I as a writer? That was my job. I was going to have to let the wisdom – or lack thereof – flow more organically from my mind. I couldn't force it.

I made a casino trip.

I spent a day sitting in the nearby café chatting with the locals.

I walked along the riverbank picking up stones and tossing them into the water. A couple of them I kept to bring home and put on a shelf as a reminder of where I'd been.

That was when it came to me. It was the perfect metaphor for my itinerant life. Picking up stones. Considering the relative merits of each one. Its cracks and flaws. Its color and striations. The smoothness of time and the crevices wrought by catastrophe. The ones I chose to keep and to treasure were my milestones. These were the objects I would not forget. On the flat surface of one large stone I would write in indelible marker, "Mckenzie River, 2020."

It came to me again that this forest was where I had chosen to have my ashes strewn when I am dead. I had made a good choice. The light here, sheeting through the trees, was surreal. I could see things here that were invisible to me in the civilized world. Perhaps my stones will carry some of their refracted light with them to light up my bedroom when I am home. Perhaps I will in time become a part of that light, dappling the leaves on overhanging branches with its magic.

I had a long mental list of things to do when I returned to the city. Consult a lawyer to draw up a will. Develop a book proposal for my memoir. Start hunting for an agent to represent me. Call around and try to kick-start the rescue business. Schedule my radiation treatment. There was much to be done. It all started to weigh heavily on my mind as I continued to fine-tune my manuscript. Mentally, I was already half-way back to town. But it was okay. So long as there were things to accomplish, I would keep myself going. That was the point of life and it had sustained me thus far. It was really a beautiful system and I continued to chug along like the old train that ran across the trestle over the river.

When I arrived back home, I felt refreshed and ready to begin again. I tackled my to-do list with renewed gusto. Soon there was only one item left on it. Schedule my radiation treatment. I had hemmed and hawed long enough. The time had come. I put down the dog-eared list and picked up my phone to call the doctor's office.

ACKNOWLEDGEMENTS

I wish to acknowledge the following journals for their support in publishing parts of this book as standalone essays:

RavensPerch, Decline, April 2020.

Free State Review, Scrapping the Memoir, August 2020.

Summerset Review, My Mother's War, September 2020.

Drunk Monkeys, Traveling Without Men, July 2021.

And because it really does take a village, I offer a big THANK YOU to each of the following for their encouragement and assistance:

Lisa Caradine – My brilliant and lovely daughter, for putting up with my menagerie and my odd writerly ways.

Sharon Harmon – Executive director at Oregon Humane Society in Portland, Oregon, for giving me the focus I needed to start Other Mothers Animal Rescue.

Cheryl Holland – Renaissance woman and friend, for challenging me gently to further my knowledge of the craft.

Chi Nelson – Photographer, for her skills that made me look a little less of a goober in my website photos.

<u>Natalie Serber</u> – Writer and teacher, whose memoir bootcamp at Literary Arts got me up and running on this project.

<u>Scarlet, Sophie, Blancmange and Pilkington</u> – Homebodies, for serving as my loyal muses and mentors.

<u>Darin Short</u> – Web developer extraordinaire, for creating my author website as well as the original website for Other Mothers Animal Rescue.

<u>Everyone at Unsolicited Press</u> – For invaluable guidance, hand holding and professionalism.

<u>Barrett Warner</u> - General editor at *Free State Review*, for tirelessly editing my book manuscript and offering countless ideas to make it better.

<u>Cynthia Whitcomb</u> – Writer and teacher, whose experience and instruction at sea inspired me to try to be a "real" writer.

ABOUT THE AUTHOR

Linda Caradine is a Portland, Oregon based writer of fiction and nonfiction. Her articles and stories have been included in numerous magazines and newspapers. Additionally, her essays have appeared extensively in the literary journals, including The RavensPerch, Summerset Review, Free State Review, Cobalt Review, Iris Literary Journal, Lowestoft Chronicle, 45th Parallel, Adelaide, Down in the Dirt, Drunk Monkeys, and others. She has won first place in the Edmunds (Washington) Arts Commission's competition for Short Fiction with an account of a fantastical encounter with Bigfoot in rural Oregon.

When she is not writing, Linda manages a nonprofit animal rescue organization that she started in 2005. She is a past winner of the Oregon Humane Society's prestigious Diamond Collar Award for her leadership in the field of animal welfare. Animals have always been one of her life's passions.

ABOUT THE PRESS

Unsolicited Press is based out of Portland, Oregon and focuses on the works of the unsung and underrepresented. As a womxn-owned, all-volunteer small publisher that doesn't worry about profits as much as championing exceptional literature, we have the privilege of partnering with authors skirting the fringes of the lit world. We've worked with emerging and award-winning authors such as Shann Ray, Amy Shimshon-Santo, Brook Bhagat, Kris Amos, and John W. Bateman.

Learn more at unsolicitedpress.com. Find us on twitter and instagram.